COUNTRIES OF THE WORLD

South Korea

Gareth Stevens Publishing
A WORLD ALMANAC EDUCATION GROUP COMPANY

About the Author: Johanna Masse was
born in Seoul, South Korea, but grew up in
Massachusetts, U.S. She currently lives in Los
Angeles, California, where she is a freelance
writer and editor specializing in Asian and
Asian-American history.

Written by
JOHANNA MASSE

Edited by
LEONG WEN SHAN

Edited in the U.S. by
MARY DYKSTRA
MONICA RAUSCH

Designed by
ROSIE FRANCIS

Picture research by
SUSAN JANE MANUEL

First published in North America in 2002 by
Gareth Stevens Publishing
A World Almanac Education Group Company
330 West Olive Street, Suite 100
Milwaukee, Wisconsin 53212 USA

Please visit our web site at
www.garethstevens.com
For a free color catalog describing
Gareth Stevens Publishing's list of high-quality
books and multimedia programs, call 1-800-542-2595
or fax your request to (414) 332-3567.

© **TIMES MEDIA PRIVATE LIMITED 2002**
Originated and designed by
Times Editions
An imprint of Times Media Private Limited
A member of the Times Publishing Group
Times Centre, 1 New Industrial Road
Singapore 536196
http://www.timesone.com.sg/te

Library of Congress Cataloging-in-Publication Data
Masse, Johanna, 1976–
South Korea / by Johanna Masse.
p. cm — (Countries of the world)
Summary: Provides an overview of the geography, history,
government, daily life, language, art, and food of South Korea,
as well as exploring its customs and current issues.
Includes bibliographical references and index.
ISBN 0-8368-2353-2 (lib. bdg.)
1. Korea (South)—Juvenile literature.
2. Korea (South)—Civilization—Juvenile literature.
[1. Korea (South)] I. Title.
II. Countries of the world (Milwaukee, Wis.)
DS902.M286   2002
951.95—dc21   2002017574

Printed in Malaysia

1 2 3 4 5 6 7 8 9 06 05 04 03 02

PICTURE CREDITS
A.N.A. Press Agency: 13, 58, 64, 65 (top)
Art Directors & TRIP Photographic Library:
    4, 21, 23, 25, 28, 47, 68 (top)
Camera Press: 5, 17, 60, 65 (bottom), 80
Downtown MoneyPoint: 90
Alain Evrard: 1, 3 (center), 9 (bottom), 18,
    19, 20, 41 (both), 48, 49 (both), 55, 68
    (bottom), 70, 74
Focus Team – Italy: 7, 38, 40, 66
Getty Images/HultonArchive: 14, 15
    (bottom), 37, 50, 51, 75, 77, 82, 83, 84
Haga Library, Japan: cover, 3 (bottom), 22,
    35 (both), 42, 43, 54, 56, 57, 62, 87, 91
HBL Network Photo Agency: 24, 45
    (bottom), 52
The Hutchison Library: 63, 89
Korea National Tourism Organization: 3
    (top), 8, 9 (top), 10, 11, 15 (top), 16, 26,
    27 (top), 29, 30, 33, 34, 36, 39, 44, 45
    (top), 59, 67, 69, 72, 73, 81
Earl and Nazima Kowall: 79
Lonely Planet Images: 78
North Wind Picture Archives: 12, 27
    (bottom), 76
Scanpix: 61
Kay Shaw Photography: 2, 6, 31, 46, 71
Topham Picturepoint: 32, 53, 85

Digital Scanning by Superskill Graphics Pte Ltd

Contents

4

AN OVERVIEW OF SOUTH KOREA

Korea has traditionally been considered a quiet and mysterious country in Eastern Asia. Overshadowed by its Chinese and Japanese neighbors in ancient times, the Korean peninsula was known as the "Hermit Kingdom." Culturally, the peninsula has been influenced by its neighbors, but this geographic location between China and the Japanese islands has also often led to war. As a result of the Korean War (1950–1953), the peninsula is now divided into two countries: the Democratic People's Republic of Korea, or North Korea, and the Republic of Korea, or South Korea.

Although divided, the people of Korea have persevered in creating a unique culture. South Korea is prospering in the global economy, and, today, it clearly is no longer a hermit nation.

Opposite: **These structures form part of the fortress walls that surrounded the capital of Korea during the Yi dynasty (1392–1910). They acted as a first line of defense against foreign enemies.**

Below: **Korean children dressed in traditional costumes celebrate at an agricultural festival.**

THE FLAG OF THE COUNTRY

The South Korean flag, also known as *t'aegukki* (tie-gook-ee), reflects much of the philosophy that lies deep within Korean culture. The perfectly divided red and blue circle symbolizes balance in the universe. The groups of black lines are called trigrams. The trigram in the upper left-hand corner represents heaven. Diagonally, the trigram in the bottom right-hand corner stands for earth, while the trigram in the upper right-hand corner and its diagonal trigram symbolize water and fire, respectively. These opposite symbols counter one another and create overall harmony.

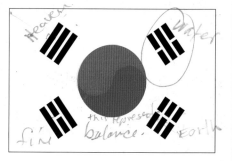

Geography

The Korean peninsula juts east off the Asian continent and occupies an area of 84,300 square miles (218,337 square kilometers). The border between North and South Korea is known as the Demilitarized Zone, or DMZ. South Korea occupies 37,900 square miles (98,161 square km) and is bordered by the Sea of Japan to the east and the Yellow Sea to the west. Off its coasts are thousands of tiny islands — actually the tops of underwater mountains — that also belong to South Korea.

Rivers

Rivers in South Korea tend to be broad and shallow with variable water flow depending on the season. These rivers are crucial for irrigating the nation's farms, while dams along the rivers provide a source of hydroelectricity. The longest river in South Korea, the Naktong, is over 325 miles (523 km) long and flows from north to south, emptying into the Korea Strait. Only slightly shorter is the Han River, which flows through Seoul — the country's capital — and empties into the Yellow Sea.

CHEJU

Cheju, South Korea's largest island, is located southwest of the peninsula. This island is home to Mount Halla, the country's highest mountain, at 6,398 feet (1,950 meters).
(A Closer Look, page 48)

Below: Flowing for 319 miles (513 km), the Han River is an important transportation route.

Mountains and Lowlands

Much of the Korean peninsula is extremely rugged and mountainous, particularly in the north. The eastern coast is much smoother than the jagged southern and western coasts. The two major mountain ranges in South Korea are the Taebaek range along the northeastern coast and the Sobaek range, which runs from north to south through the middle of South Korea. Mount Chiri, at 6,283 feet (1,915 m), is the highest mountain on the South Korean mainland.

Some of the land in the mountains is arable, but most of it is covered with forests. Before conservation efforts, Koreans cut down many of the country's forests for farming and firewood, which led to soil erosion and flooding. In the 1960s, intensive reforestation programs began. Today, most of the forest has been recovered, and the foliage is lush.

Only thirty percent of South Korea's total area is considered lowland. The existing lowland can be found primarily along the country's southern and western coasts.

Above: **Soraksan National Park in Kangwon Province is a favorite spot for mountain climbers, due to its stunning scenery that changes with each passing season.**

Climate

South Korea has four distinct seasons and a humid climate that is affected by the peninsula's topographical features.

Warm, sunny spring weather arrives in April. Summer comes in June, and from June to September, the monsoon from the south brings hot, humid air to the mainland. In July and August, the average temperature soars to about 78° Fahrenheit (26° Celsius); at this time, reprieves from the heat can only be found in the cool mountains. Winter is generally mild, with January being the coldest month of the year. In January, the average minimum temperature in Seoul is 15° F (-9° C). Temperatures tend to be warmer in the southern part of the peninsula.

Monsoon winds also bring heavy rain. Summer is the rainy season, during which almost half the annual precipitation falls. Between June and August, some parts of Korea receive over 30 inches (76 centimeters) of rain. Humidity is highest in July. Flooding and property damage sometimes occur when tropical typhoons hit the mainland in late summer. Droughts plague South Korea about once a decade.

Below: **The Secret Garden of Changdok Palace in Seoul contains a beautiful pond and a banquet pavilion, which were previously used by its royal inhabitants.**

Left: **The Rose of Sharon — South Korea's national flower — blooms throughout the summer.**

Plants and Animals

South Korea is rich in vegetation, mainly due to its temperate climate and rich soil. Both evergreen and deciduous trees, such as maple, oak, and birch, fill the many forests on the peninsula. Fir, pine, spruce, and other hardy coniferous species thrive in the mountains, while more delicate citrus trees grow along the southern coast. Fruit trees include apple and pear, as well as the more exotic Chinese quince. Taegu is known as the apple capital of the country. The oldest fruit-bearing tree in the world can be found at Yongmun-sa temple in Kyonggi province; it is a mighty ginkgo tree, planted in the tenth century by a prince during the Silla dynasty. In July and August, the warmest months of the year, flowers all over the peninsula burst into bloom.

In the past, South Korea was home to a large variety of forest-dwelling mammals. Human development has encroached on the natural habitats of the bears, tigers, and leopards that used to roam the peninsula. These creatures have dwindled in number over the years. Smaller mammals, such as weasels, continue to thrive. Cheju, the southernmost point in South Korea, is richest in both plant and animal life, including the Cheju pony, which was, historically, used for agricultural purposes.

Below: **The Korean tiger, which used to roam the nation's forests in great numbers, is the subject of many traditional paintings.**

History

Archaeological evidence shows that the Korean peninsula was inhabited by nomads as early as the Paleolithic era. Fearing the potential power of these wandering tribes, Chinese troops invaded Korea during the Chinese Han dynasty and dominated northern Korea for four hundred years (108 B.C. to A.D. 313).

The Three Kingdoms

Beginning in the first century B.C., Koreans began forming their own kingdoms, which grew more powerful as the Han dynasty weakened. The Koguryo Kingdom in the north was very militaristic, while the Silla and Paekche Kingdoms located in the south were less aggressive. These three kingdoms dominated the peninsula from the late third to mid-seventh centuries — known as the Three Kingdoms era — until Silla conquered Koguryo and Paekche in 668. The *Samguk sagi* (*History of the Three Kingdoms*) and the *Samguk yusa* (*Memorabilia of the Three Kingdoms*) both chronicled the events of this period.

Left: The Silla Cultural Festival features a parade that is a reenactment of the royal procession in the Silla Kingdom.

Left: The Chomsongdae Observatory at Kyongju, the world's oldest existing observatory in the Far East, was built during Queen Sondok's reign (A.D. 632–647).

Unification

In 668, the Silla Kingdom allied with China to defeat Koguryo and Paekche. Silla kings then ruled a unified Korea for over 250 years. The capital of Silla — present-day Kyongju — had a population of over one million people and became the fourth largest city in ancient civilization.

As the central government's power in Silla decreased, individual families grew increasingly powerful. In 918, a regional warlord named Wang Kon defeated Silla's king Kyong Myong and established his own kingdom, known as the Koryo Kingdom. The Koryo period, which lasted until 1392, was a time of great scholarship and liberal values, when women enjoyed inheritance rights that were equal to men. The name "Korea" is believed to come from this era.

In 1392, Koryo general Yi Song-gye overthrew the Koryo king and established the Yi dynasty. Korea was renamed Choson (meaning "Land of Morning Calm"), and the Yi, or Choson, dynasty lasted until 1910. Confucianism was the most important state religion during this period, and, as a result, Korean society became increasingly ranked by class and gender.

SEOUL

General Yi Song-gye, founder of the Yi dynasty, made his capital at Hanyang. The city gradually came to be known as Seoul (a Korean word meaning "capital"). General Yi, who later became King Yi Taejo, built a fortress wall with nine gates to protect the city. The remains of these gates still exist in Seoul.

(A Closer Look, page 70)

Foreign Powers and Colonial Rule

In 1894, the Choson government faced the Tonghak uprising, in which Koreans demanded reform. Both Chinese and Japanese troops were sent to help the Korean government. A confrontation between the two foreign powers led to the First Sino-Japanese War (1894–1895). China lost the war in 1895, and Japan took control of Korea's internal security. In 1905, Russia lost a war against Japan in a similar bid to control Korea. Japan then dissolved the Korean army in 1907, formally annexed the peninsula in 1910, and ruled it for thirty-five years.

Colonial rule did not end with Japan's defeat at the end of World War II in 1945. After the war, the two foreign powers who helped defeat Japan — the United States and the Soviet Union — divided the Korean peninsula into two zones of occupation, with the north under Soviet control and the south under U.S. control.

Above: **This illustration shows Japanese military forces landing in Korea in 1904.**

The Korean War (1950–1953)

On June 25, 1950, North Korean troops, aided by the Soviet Union, invaded South Korea. The United States, prompted by the United Nations Security Council, led an international effort to assist the South Korean army. This military action escalated into three years of fighting and was known as the Korean War. Almost

three years of fighting and was known as the Korean War. Almost three million Koreans and foreign nationals allied with either North or South Korea were killed. In addition, many Korean families were forced to leave their homes and resettle throughout the peninsula. A truce was signed in 1953.

Social and Political Struggle

The first president of South Korea, Syngman Rhee — backed by the United States for his conservative stance toward communism — was ousted in 1960 amid protests of government corruption. General Park Chung Hee led a military coup and seized control of the government in 1961. Park dissolved the National Assembly and imposed martial law, or control of the state by the military. He was assassinated in 1979, but his death was followed by tighter controls under various military dictators. The Korean people began launching protests and workers' strikes as their dissatisfaction grew. Military rule officially ended in 1981.

THE DMZ AND PANMUNJOM

As a result of the cease-fire agreement in 1953, the Korean peninsula was permanently divided by a stretch of land 2.5 miles (4 km) wide. This land is known as the Demilitarized Zone (DMZ). The village of Panmunjom is located along the DMZ.
(A Closer Look, page 52)

KWANGJU MASSACRE

In South Korea, university students have often demonstrated to express their dissatisfaction with the ruling government. Sometimes, student demonstrations have led to violent clashes with the police.
(A Closer Look, page 64)

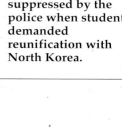

Left: A student rally held on August 15, 1996, to celebrate the anniversary of Korea's liberation from the Japanese was suppressed by the police when students demanded reunification with North Korea.

13

Plans for Reunification

During the 1990s, South Korea became an industrial powerhouse. At the same time, North Korea and South Korea began discussing the possibility of reunification. Since the collapse of the Soviet Union in 1991, North Korea has been plagued with economic and agricultural stagnation. In the late 1990s, when hundreds of thousands of North Koreans began dying of starvation, South Korea pledged aid to its former enemy.

On June 13, 2000, South Korean president Kim Dae Jung met his North Korean counterpart, President Kim Jong-il, in P'yongyang, the capital of North Korea. This was the first time such a gesture had occurred on the peninsula in fifty years. One hundred South Korean families were allowed to visit their relatives in North Korea during the three-day summit. These families were chosen by lottery, and those who "won" were able to visit family members they had not seen since 1950. Koreans throughout the peninsula celebrated this event because it marked the beginning of the path toward reunification.

KIM DAE JUNG: PRISONER TO PRESIDENT

South Korean president Kim Dae Jung was awarded the 2000 Nobel Peace Prize for his efforts toward reunifying the two Korean nations.

(A Closer Look, page 60)

Left: **Ministers from North Korea (*left*) and South Korea (*right*) meet to discuss plans for reunification.**

Queen Sondok (? – A.D. 647)

One of Korea's most enlightened queens, Queen Sondok ruled Silla Kingdom from 632 to 647. She was a great champion of knowledge and inter-Asiatic relations. Due to the good relations Queen Sondok fostered with China, Korean students were able to study in China and learn from Chinese scientists. The remains of the oldest observatory in the Far East, built during Queen Sondok's reign, still exist in Kyongju today. In addition, Queen Sondok also supported Western missionaries in directing the course of women's education.

Admiral Yi Sun-shin (1545–1598)

Korea's greatest hero is probably Admiral Yi Sun-shin. Admiral Yi invented the world's first ironclad warships, known as "turtleboats" for their defensive powers. The turtleboats helped avert a Japanese invasion during the Yi dynasty as they were unlike anything the enemy had expected. When the Japanese tried to land their ships on the Korean coasts, Admiral Yi managed to defeat them, even though his fleets were often greatly outnumbered. Fighting to the end, Admiral Yi died during the Japanese retreat. Koreans honor him today as an excellent military tactician and honorable gentleman.

Admiral Yi Sun-shin

Park Chung Hee (1917–1979)

Between 1960 and 1961, South Korea experienced severe economic problems. Political and social uncertainty led the military, headed by General Park Chung Hee, to step in and establish martial law. Park subsequently took over the government as head of state. His aggressive efforts in obtaining foreign capital effectively improved the nation's economy; shipyards, steel mills, and electronic factories transformed South Korea's previously agricultural landscape into an industrial one. The nation's per capita income, or income earned by each person, increased tenfold during his presidency. Park's supporters, however, decreased as he began to suppress civil rights. During a heated government discussion on October 26, 1979, Park Chung Hee was assassinated by the head of the Korean Central Intelligence Agency (KCIA).

Park Chung Hee

Government and the Economy

Government Structure

South Korea is a democracy. The South Korean government has three branches: executive, legislative, and judicial. The president is head of the executive branch; a prime minister and various executive councils serve under the president.

Presidential elections are held every five years, and all South Koreans over the age of twenty can vote. A president can only serve one five-year term. The president acts as the head of South Korea's foreign relations and is the commander-in-chief of the armed forces. The prime minister is chosen by the president to oversee the daily workings of the government. The president's choice has to be approved by the legislature. The prime minister then recommends deputy prime ministers and fifteen to thirty state council members to help with various tasks. The president appoints these positions based on the recommendations put forward by the prime minister.

Left: **The National Assembly building in Seoul provides various facilities for the legislative members to carry out their tasks.**

Left: **Although military rule officially ended in 1981, military officials continued to orchestrate government elections until 1992, when South Koreans elected Kim Young Sam. Kim was the first civilian president since 1961.**

South Korea's legislature is known as the National Assembly and is made up of 273 seats. Most representatives of the assembly (227) are elected for four-year terms by popular vote; the remaining seats are divided among the political parties. The assembly is responsible for proposing and enacting (or rejecting) new laws, endorsing foreign treaties, approving the president's choice for prime minister, and overseeing government agencies. The National Assembly also approves the president's appointees to the Supreme Court. The major political parties in South Korea are the Grand National Party (GNP), the Millennium Democratic Party (MDP), and the United Liberal Democrats (ULD). President Kim Dae Jung is a member of the MDP.

The judiciary branch consists of three levels: the Supreme Court, five appellate courts, and district courts. The Supreme Court has the final word on decisions made in the lesser courts. The president appoints a chief justice and other justices to serve in the Supreme Court for six-year terms.

CITIES AND PROVINCES

South Korea is divided into nine major provinces for administrative purposes. Seven cities — Seoul, Inch'on, Kwangju, Taejon, Pusan, Taegu, and Ulsan — have independent local governments.

Economy

When the Japanese controlled the Korean peninsula, they developed agriculture in the south and industry in the north. When the peninsula was split, South Korea was then left with limited industrial resources. During its first years as an independent nation, the economy of South Korea struggled.

Over the years, the country has built a strong industrial base for itself, and it is now known as one of the "Four Dragons of East Asia." Today, South Korea's gross national product (GNP) — the total value of goods and services produced during a year — rivals those of many small European countries. The government's careful monitoring of business growth through the late 1980s is largely responsible for this success, which has revolutionized the former "Hermit Kingdom."

Manufacturing Sector

Some of the strongest industries in South Korea are electronics, automobile production, chemicals, shipbuilding, steel, clothing, shoes, and food processing.

COMPUTER CHIPS AND CYBER GAMES

South Korea is at the forefront of many high-tech industries, including the production of computer chips. The country's Internet-savvy younger generation enjoys playing online games, also known as cyber games.
(*A Closer Look, page 50*)

Below: Although life in the countryside is not as modernized as in the city, the use of advanced agricultural methods enables Korean farmers to get maximum yields.

THE LABOR FORCE

Part of South Korea's economic success is attributed to its large, highly educated, and relatively inexpensive labor force. The country's large cities, such as Seoul and Pusan, teem with residents and migrant workers from the surrounding countryside who fill the ranks of Korea's labor force. Most Koreans work six days a week.

South Korea's major exports are electronics, cars, clothing, and fish. The United States is the biggest importer of Korean goods. South Korea imports chemicals, machinery, oil, grains, and other raw materials. In January 2002, South Korea enjoyed a trade surplus of $180 million.

South Korea's industrial boom has also created increased urbanization. Rising demand for new buildings, houses, and transportation routes provides a steady source of employment for construction companies.

Agricultural Sector

Only about 12 percent of the population is involved in agriculture. South Korea's major crops are rice, barley, and vegetables, and major livestock include cattle, pigs, chickens, and fish. Most of the farms in South Korea are small and privately owned. Because the amount of arable land in South Korea is so limited, large-scale farming is impractical, if not impossible. South Korea's climate is ideal for growing rice — the principal crop — and over half the farmland is devoted to this staple. Many farmers supplement their income by fishing.

NATURAL RESOURCES

Since South Korea lacks natural resources, Korean industries often exchange finished goods for raw materials when trading with countries such as the United States, Japan, and China. South Korea's current trade surplus shows that this strategy has worked well.

People and Lifestyle

Korea's Homogeneous Ethnic Origins

Koreans are thought to be descendents of several Mongol tribes that migrated from present-day Manchuria (northeastern China) to the Korean peninsula in prehistoric times. Today, South Korea is one of the most densely populated countries in the world, with close to 48 million citizens. Most Koreans speak the same language and share similar cultural backgrounds.

Very few non-Koreans have settled in South Korea. The largest non-Korean ethnic population is Chinese, but they account for only about twenty thousand people.

Over three-quarters of all South Koreans live in cities. Because so much of the peninsula is mountainous, many areas are uninhabited. Therefore, the population is concentrated along the western coast and the banks of the nation's rivers.

HANBOK: TRADITIONAL COSTUME

Koreans are influenced by both traditional and Western values. While many Koreans usually wear jeans and sneakers or suits and dresses, on holidays or special occasions they may dress in their traditional clothing.
(A Closer Look, page 56)

Left: The majority of South Korea's population shares the same cultural heritage.

Left: **The modern Korean home is a mixture of the old and new; families enjoy watching television while eating on their traditional low tables and sitting on heated floors.**

To accommodate the nation's limited space for growth, the government initiated a family planning program in 1962. Today, the population growth rate is less than 1 percent per year. The male to female ratio is even, and the average life expectancy is seventy-four years of age.

Korean Homes

Korean homes are traditionally small, one-story, L-shaped dwellings with tiled roofs. Inside, they contain a kitchen, living room, and bedroom. Sometimes, screens are used in the bigger rooms to provide privacy. Rooms were once heated with a unique *ondol* (on-doll) system invented during the fourth century B.C.; ducts under the floor projected heat from the kitchen fire into the other rooms. Modern Korean homes in both the cities and countryside continue to use the ondol system, but, instead of firewood, gas or electricity is used to heat water pipes under the floor. Floors are made of clay and stone, as these materials conduct heat well. Shoes are usually not worn in a Korean home.

Traditionally, the rooms are sparsely furnished and often do not have tables and chairs because everyone sits on the heated floors. Recently, however, the use of Western-style furniture has also gained popularity among Korean homemakers.

TRANSPORTATION

As most people do not own cars, South Korea has an efficient system of public transportation and railroads that allows Koreans to travel around the country conveniently.

Family Life

The family is and always has been the center of a Korean's outlook and philosophy. Traditional Korean families were governed according to Confucian values, which prize family harmony over the individual member's will. Households were very large in traditional Korea, consisting of many generations of family members, as well as servants. When sons married, they brought their brides home to live with their parents. Extensive households employed servants to help with the chores. By obeying the Confucian social order, everyone understood who had authority, and this allowed large numbers of people to live together harmoniously.

In the Past

The traditional Korean lifestyle was restrictive for young people and women. Men, particularly the father or grandfather, were at the heads of the household, and the rest of the family obeyed their

Below: **In traditional Korean weddings, elaborate ceremonies such as ancestor worship have to be observed.**

Left: **Nuclear families, consisting of a father, a mother, and their children, are common in cities throughout South Korea.**

wishes. Unmarried men and women were treated as children and wore their hair parted in the middle and plaited into braids. Boys and girls were separated at a young age, and girls could not leave the house.

In the Present

Some of South Korea's ancient customs were discontinued as the country progressed into a modern nation. Today, boys and girls have equal opportunities since status is no longer determined by gender. Elders are still given the highest respect, but generational roles are not strictly enforced. Men and women work both in and out of the home. People marry for love, not according to astrological forecasts and not necessarily according to their parents' wishes. Families are small and usually consist of only the parents and their children. Comparatively, families in rural areas tend to be more traditional than those living in the cities.

Education

Historically, Koreans have placed a great deal of importance on education. This emphasis can be traced back to Korea's ancient roots as a Confucian society, when government posts were determined by competitive examinations. These examinations involved studying and memorizing ancient classical texts. Until the late 1800s, only boys from wealthy families attended school.

When missionaries arrived from Western countries in the nineteenth century, they brought new ideas about education. Students learned a wide variety of subjects, such as the English language, mathematics, and science. Today, all Koreans have an equal opportunity to receive education.

Structure of Education

The South Korean educational system is divided into four levels: six years of elementary school, three years of middle school, three years of high school, and four years of college. Elementary school and middle school are compulsory, free of charge, and designed to provide every citizen with basic literacy. Since the 1960s, the

FEMALE EDUCATION

In 1886, Methodist missionary Mary Scranton bought a piece of land in Seoul and established Ewha Haktang, the first Korean school devoted entirely to the education of women.

government has provided free textbooks to elementary school students to promote equality in their learning experiences.

High school builds on skills developed in middle school with an eye toward the student's future career goals. High schools are either academic or vocational in curriculum and tend to be single-sex. Academic schools offer a mixture of required courses, optional or selected courses, and extracurricular activities. Students in their second year can choose to major in the humanities and social sciences, natural sciences, or vocational training. The vocational high school curriculum includes training in agriculture, technology, and commerce. South Koreans have won numerous awards in international vocational training competitions, such as the World Skills competition organized by the International Vocational Training Organization (IVTO).

The government regulates the number of students who go on to either two-year junior colleges or four-year colleges. Since 1969, prospective college students have been required to take a qualifying state examination for college entrance. The intent is to prevent poorly educated high school students from entering college. After passing the state exams, students must then pass the entrance exams of the individual universities. More than half of all high school graduates enroll at a college or university.

MIDDLE SCHOOL ENTRANCE EXAM

Previously, students had to take an examination to progress into middle school. Studying for the examination, however, was so stressful for the students that the government abolished the requirement.

Left: An elementary school teacher instructs a class of students. Elementary school is only the beginning of a student's educational career, which can last up to sixteen years.

Religion: Shamanistic Beginnings

Ancient Koreans believed that spirits resided in natural forces and inanimate objects, such as trees or the earth itself. This attempt to come to terms with unfathomable events in nature is known as shamanism, an early and primitive religion. A shaman is a magician or priest who mediates between the human and spirit worlds. Some Koreans have continued to practice this folk religion, often praying for cures for illnesses or for good harvests.

Buddhism

More a philosophy than a religion, Buddhism reached Korea around A.D. 370. By this time, Buddhism had evolved into a form called Mahayana Buddhism. As the official state religion of the Silla dynasty, Buddhist influences can often be observed in the art and cultural movements of that time. Today, Buddhism remains one of the most popular religions practiced by South Koreans, and many South Koreans celebrate Buddhist festivals.

BUDDHIST TENETS

Buddhists believe that sorrow comes from wanting what one does not or cannot have. Until people realize this futility, they are destined to be endlessly reincarnated, or reborn, into different life forms. Through Buddhist practice, one can break free from the cycle of reincarnation.

Below: **This procession of Buddhist monks was held on the Buddha's birthday.**

Confucianism

Confucianism is not a religion whereby people believe in and worship a god or several gods. Instead, it involves a complex system of relationships designed to promote order in society. Its system is based on a respect for social order and a willingness to obey those higher in rank. In Korea, Confucianism was once essential in governing all relationships.

Christianity

Christianity has become one of South Korea's largest religions. The religion first came to Korea through diplomats traveling from China in the seventeenth century. The Korean monarchs did not approve of this foreign religion, and in the 1800s, thousands of its followers were persecuted and killed. A diplomatic treaty with the United States in 1882 provided protection for missionaries, and various Protestant denominations consequently began sending ministers, medical personnel, and educators to the Korean peninsula.

Below: **Confucius was a Chinese sage who developed an ethical system designed to ideally govern all relationships in the family, the community, and the state.**

CONFUCIUS.

Language and Literature

Language scholars believe that in ancient times the Korean, Chinese, and Japanese languages developed and spread from a single central Asian source. Unlike Chinese, which has many different dialects, the Korean language has only six dialects. Although they vary in tone and grammar, all these dialects are intelligible to one another. The present official Korean language is modeled on the dialect that was spoken in and around Seoul in the 1930s.

Sijo and Pansori

Sijo (see-joe), a type of short, lyrical poem practiced by the nobility and the wealthy, gained popularity during the Koryo dynasty. Usually three lines long and often containing a clever hidden meaning, sijo changed according to the social, political, and cultural atmosphere of the time. Common people enjoyed *pansori* (pahn-sore-ee) during the Koryo period, which are folktales describing the virtues and concerns of everyday life,

HANGUL AND KING SEJONG

King Sejong's rule (1419–1450) was a golden era in which cultural arts, science, education, and commerce flourished. The sundial and astronomical maps were developed, and one of the world's first encyclopedias was written during his reign. Perhaps King Sejong's greatest achievement was the creation of Korea's official written language, *hangul* (hahn-gool).
(A Closer Look, page 58)

Left: **Signs in South Korea are often written in hangul and English.**

Left: **This monument shows a poem by Sambong Jeong Do-jeon who was a scholar and a reformer in the Choson dynasty.**

often set to music. The themes in pansori often embody a mixture of Buddhist, Confucian, and shamanistic beliefs.

Historical Records

Koreans' knowledge of their ancient history is chiefly derived from two texts: the *Samguk sagi* by Kim Pu-sik (1075–1151) and the *Samguk yusa* by the monk Iryon (1206–1289). These texts contained folktales, legends, songs, and shamanist prayers.

Contemporary Literature

Modern Korean literature tends to reflect the trauma and upheaval of recent Korean history. The most famous poet of the early twentieth century is Kim So-wol, who wrote mostly about nature. He was strongly influenced by European writers, and his poem "Azalea" is one of the most famous Korean poems in the twentieth century. Other writers, such as Kim Chi-ha, used poetry to convey their disenchantment with the government. Park Kyong-ni wrote about Korea under Japanese rule; during this period, Korean writing tended to have a sorrowful tone. In a poll conducted in 2001, Park's eight-volume novel, *Land*, published in 1969, was considered by Korean intellectuals to be most representative of Korean literature.

Arts

Ritual Dance

Korean dance has evolved from the culture's agricultural roots. The three main kinds of traditional Korean dances include ritual, folk, and court dances.

The most common ritual dances are derived from Confucian and Buddhist customs. These dances have been passed down through the generations as temple traditions and preserved in their original form.

Buddhist dancers usually wear white or yellow robes. The rhythms of their dances often portray the conflict between the physical and spiritual worlds. One Buddhist ritual dance is the drum dance, in which a young priest wearing a hood and beating a drum performs before an image of Buddha.

MASK DANCES

Korean masks are called *tal* (tall), and mask dances are known as *talchum* (tall-choom). Early mask dance dramas were generally religious in nature. The themes became increasingly secular as Korean society grew more complex. (*A Closer Look, page 68*)

Below: **Ritual dances of ancestral worship are still widely performed by Koreans today.**

Folk Dance

Folk dancing is exciting and exuberant, with an emphasis on energy and color. One of the most popular folk dances is the farmer's dance. During agricultural festivals, the male farmers of a village gather together under a flag to celebrate the importance of farming. The dancers wear brightly colored costumes and hats decorated with long white streamers. Accompanied by drums and brass instruments, the men spin through the air, whipping their necks from side to side so the streamers float. The emphasis on neck movements is a unique feature of the Korean farmer's dance. As industry becomes more important, Koreans perform the farmer's dance to remind themselves that agriculture has been the backbone of their country.

Above: **The bright costumes and the vibrancy of the farmer's dance make the performance an exciting event.**

Court Dance

Most folk dances are athletic in nature compared to the stately court dances. While folk dances are animated, fast in tempo, and unrestrained, court dances tend to be more complex, restricted, and elegant. In the past, the nobility often celebrated feasts or major events with court dances as entertainment. Child dancers performed to a mixture of music and song. A narrator usually described the theme of the dance to the audience.

SWORD DANCE

Women may perform the sword dance, in which one or many women dance around holding a sword in each hand. The dance is graceful and feminine and does not require skilled swordsmanship.

Music

In the past, villagers used materials they found around them, such as bamboo, string, wood, and stones, to create musical instruments. People probably used music and dance to celebrate the harvest or to perform rituals. Hundreds of traditional folk songs are part of South Korea's oral tradition; the songs vary from village to village and are passed from one generation to the next.

The two most prominent instruments in traditional Korean music are the *komungo* (koh-moon-go) and the *kayagum* (kie-yah-goom). The komungo was invented in the fourth century and modeled after the Chinese zither. The original komungo had four strings and sixteen movable bridges. A musician played the instrument by plucking the strings with a small stick known as a plectrum. The kayagum is a twelve-stringed zither that was developed around the sixth century. Another well-loved instrument among the Korean people is the *changgo* (chahng-go), or hourglass drum. The changgo was usually used to provide rhythm for dances. The musician would hang the changgo around his or her neck and then strike the two ends of the drum with sticks.

Above: A musician plays the komungo. Such traditional instruments are often played during cultural festivals. Present-day komungos have six strings.

CELADON POTTERY

Korean ceramics were largely influenced by Chinese patterns and techniques, but Korean potters raised the art form to an entirely new level. Though relatively unknown until the twentieth century, Korean celadon pottery has come to epitomize the finest achievement of Korean culture.
(A Closer Look, page 46)

Painting

The earliest examples of Korean painting are tomb murals in North Korea estimated to be more than fifteen hundred years old. The murals depict imaginary beasts, such as dragons and phoenixes — both spirits in the shaman belief system.

From the fifth century until the Yi dynasty (1392–1910), Buddhism was the primary artistic influence, and thousands of images of Buddha were carved out of bronze or stone. By the time of the Choson era, Confucianism had replaced Buddhism as the dominant cultural force. Confucian artistic pursuits included Chinese-style calligraphy and landscape painting. The paintings of Kim Chong-hui, a Confucian scholar during the 1800s, are still exhibited today. Folk art, on the other hand, was less realistic than that of the Confucian painters and more apt to incorporate Buddhist or shamanistic images. Often folk art depicted abstract ideas, such as man and nature, and used everyday symbols to express ideas such as longevity and happiness. These kinds of paintings have only recently been recognized for their contributions to Korea's cultural legacy.

Below: **Buddhist temples are often adorned with intricate artwork depicting religious figures.**

Leisure and Festivals

Traditional Games

Many Korean games originated in China and have been adapted over time. Families often enjoy these traditional pastimes during festivals and national holidays.

Two traditional board games are *changgi* (chahng-gee) and *paduk* (pah-duke). Changgi is the Korean version of Chinese chess and was historically entertainment for the common people. Each of two changgi players has sixteen pieces that represent horses, elephants, chariots, soldiers, cannons, and a general. As in chess, the goal of the game is to capture the general of the opponent. The younger or less experienced player always has the first move.

Paduk is a popular board game that originated in China. The game is played on a grid of nineteen by nineteen lines. In this strategic game, small black and white stones are placed on the board to control an area and capture the opponent's stones. Koreans dominate international paduk competitions.

Below: **While some paduk players take part in international competitions, the majority of Koreans play the game solely for pleasure.**

Left: A game of Korean-style seesaw is often played during the lunar New Year.

Flying kites is another favorite pastime in Korea, with a long legacy in Korean tradition. More than seventy different kite designs are found in South Korea. The most popular is the shield kite, made from five bamboo sticks and covered with mulberry paper, with a round hole that acts as a propeller. Today, during lunar New Year celebrations, children fly kites and then let go of the string, symbolizing the send-off of bad luck to begin the new year. The oldest existing record of kite flying involves Silla General Kim Yusin. In 647, he hung a burning straw scarecrow from a kite and sent it over enemy barracks to win a battle.

Koreans also enjoy playing on seesaws during lunar New Year celebrations. Koreans stand on their seesaws and bounce up and down. The seesaw itself is usually just a plank of wood placed on a bag of rice straw or a rolled-up mat. Seesaw has been a traditional pastime, especially among Korean women, since ancient times.

Men often play the more violent *chajonnori* (chah-john-nor-ee), in which two teams compete to knock their opponents off raised platforms. One player stands on top of a platform called a *dongchae* (dong-chay), which is made of wood and old rice stalks. The dongchae is carried by his teammates. Each team repeatedly rams into the opponent's platform. If a leader falls down or a dongchae touches the ground, the opposing side wins.

Below: Flying a shield kite is enjoyed by both the young and the elderly. According to legend, a Korean general conquered Cheju by flying his soldiers to the island via kites at the end of the Koryo dynasty.

Mountain Climbing

The most popular physical pastime in South Korea is mountain climbing. Since mountainous terrain covers 70 percent of Korea, a good climb is never too far away. Most of the mountains are low and gradual, so people of all ages and fitness levels can participate. On weekends, mountain trails are usually crowded with families and hiking clubs.

Soccer and Baseball

Soccer came to Korea in 1882, when British sailors introduced the sport to the country. South Korea was the first country in Asia to create a professional soccer team. A national league was created in 1983, which became the Korean League in 1994. The South Korean soccer team has won medals at the Asian Games several times. In 2002, South Korea and Japan co-hosted the FIFA World Cup.

A professional baseball league was established in South Korea in 1982. Younger Korean baseball players won the Little League World Series in 1984 and 1985. In 2000, the country defeated the U.S. team and won the gold medal at the AAA World Junior Baseball Championship, which was held in Canada.

Above: **Many Koreans hike to visit the Buddhist shrines located in the mountains. Most Koreans, though, hike to spend time with their friends and family while enjoying the great outdoors.**

1988 OLYMPICS

South Korea was the second Asian nation to host the Summer Olympics, after Japan.
(A Closer Look, page 44)

Archery

In earlier times, archery was the one sport that noblewomen could practice without appearing "unladylike." In the past, major competitive archery tournaments were held in spring and autumn. These were subsequently overshadowed by other sports, such as soccer and baseball. Korean women continue to excel in the sport, and Korean female archers won gold medals in both the individual and team competitions in the 1988 and 1992 Olympics.

Long-distance Running

Koreans have shown great skill in long distance running. In 1936, Sohn Kee-chung and Nam Sung-yong won the gold and bronze medals, respectively, in the marathon at the Berlin Olympics. Sohn set the Olympic record at the time, when Korea was still under Japanese control. In 1950, South Korean runners, led by Ham Kee-yong, captured first, second, and third place in the Boston Marathon, one of the most difficult and prestigious courses in the world. In 2001, Lee Bong-ju became the first Korean runner since Ham Kee-yong to win the Boston Marathon.

TAEKWONDO: A TRADITIONAL MARTIAL ART

Taekwondo originated in Korea, and many non-Koreans around the world practice the sport today. Children and adults go to *dojangs* (doh-jahns) to learn and practice this martial art. A dojang is literally a gymnasium or training hall, but, to Koreans, a dojang also suggests a place of honor where people go to study the ways of a warrior.
(*A Closer Look, page 72*)

Below: **Lee Bong-ju** (*second from left*) **pulls away from the pack to emerge as winner at the Boston Marathon.**

37

New Year Celebrations

The first major holiday in the year is New Year's Day on January 1. New Year celebrations often continue for three days in Korea. In fact, the New Year festival, known as *Solnal* (sole-nahl), is usually the biggest event of the year. During this festival, families gather, and young members show respect for their elders by bowing to their parents and older relatives, wishing them good fortune. The elders reward the children with advice for the new year and a gift of money, cakes, or fruit. Families spend this time playing traditional games and eating special foods.

National Celebrations

Many holidays in South Korea celebrate events of historical significance in Korean history. March 1 is Independence Movement Day when Koreans observe the anniversary of the March 1, 1919, Independence Movement against Japanese colonial rule. Liberation Day falls on August 15 and marks the end of Japanese rule in 1945. This date marks a double celebration in South Korea because the Korean Republic was officially established on August 15, 1948. All South Koreans, including those living overseas, honor this event.

Above: **Young children bow to their elders on New Year's Day as a sign of respect. Korean families also celebrate the beginning of the new lunar year, which usually falls at the end of January or beginning of February.**

THE LUNAR CALENDAR

Older Korean festivals tend to be based on the lunar calendar, which is calculated by the revolution of the moon around Earth. Each month is twenty-nine or thirty days long, culminating in a thirty-day "leap month" every thirty-three months. More modern holidays are set according to the familiar Western solar calendar.

Children's Day

May 5 is the celebration of Children's Day. Ceremonies, contests, and awards are held to honor children, and many parents buy gifts for their children. Television stations run special programs geared toward entertaining the young viewers. On this day, the whole country stops to treat the younger generation.

Buddha's Birthday

On the eighth day of the fourth lunar month (which usually falls in April or May), Koreans commemorate Buddha's birthday. Practicing Buddhists observe a lantern festival to mark this event by hanging up strings of paper lotus lanterns at shrines. Buddhist temples hold rituals, and people visit the temples to pray for good fortune. Mothers often pray for their children to do well in their examinations.

LEGEND OF TANGUN

Koreans celebrate *Tangun* (tahn-goon), or National Foundation Day, on October 3. Much as Rome traces its lineage back to its early founders, Koreans believe that they too have an ancient ruler dating back to prehistoric times. Tangun, the legendary father of Korea, bridged the gap between the gods and mortals.

(A Closer Look, page 66)

Left: **Buddhist followers turn out in full force at temples for the celebration of the Buddha's Birthday, which involves a lengthy procession.**

Food

A typical Korean meal consists of rice, soup, and *kimchi* (kim-chee). The one common element found in a Korean meal, as well as in meals throughout Asia, is rice. Rice is the most important crop in South Korea, and the country's cuisine has developed around it. Boiled rice dates back to the early Silla period.

Soups also play an important role in Korean cooking. Soups range from simple vegetable broths to complicated ones containing a variety of meats, shellfish, and vegetables. Some Korean soups may also be served cold.

Another unusual feature of Korean meals is the variety of side dishes that accompany the main course. These side dishes are known as *panchen* (pahn-chen) and are usually small amounts of seasoned vegetables, meats, seaweed, bean curd, or seafood. At least two or three side dishes are served with every meal. More important meals may include six to twelve dishes. When a guest

KIMCHI: A SAVORY STAPLE

Kimchi, a spicy, pickled dish, is served with most Korean meals. Usually made of cabbage, kimchi can also be made with radishes and other vegetables. Red pepper is used to make the dish very spicy.

(A Closer Look, page 62)

Below: **A typical meal in South Korea includes several small side dishes.**

Left: Koreans tend to eat a great variety of fish and seafood. Because Korea is a peninsula, seafood has always been part of its people's diet. Koreans often broil fish or make seafood stews.

GINSENG

Herbal teas made of ginseng are popular for their medicinal properties.
(A Closer Look, page 54)

Below: Throughout the world, Korean cuisine is associated with barbecue; indeed, grilled meat is a favorite among Koreans.

is present, a good host prepares a wide variety of side dishes, of which the guest is asked to partake heartily. Korean families eat three meals a day, and the number of dishes increases with each meal, with breakfast being the lightest.

Grilling is also popular among Koreans, both at home and in restaurants. A common dish that both Koreans and foreigners enjoy is *bulgogi* (bull-go-gee). Bulgogi consists of strips of marinated beef that are grilled over an open fire. Small pieces of bulgogi and a bit of rice are wrapped in lettuce leaves and eaten by hand. Korean restaurants often have individual grills at the tables so that customers can make their own bulgogi. *Galbi* (gall-bee), barbecued short ribs, is a similar dish.

After eating, Koreans may drink a cup of tea, which is thought to be an aid for digestion. They do not usually eat desserts, such as cake or cookies, after a meal. Rather, fresh fruits, including orange slices, may be served. If Koreans eat sweets, they usually do so before meals as snacks.

A CLOSER LOOK AT SOUTH KOREA

Korean history has been marked with hardship and oppression, and South Korea is often plagued by political and social upheaval. Although foreign powers have left indelible scars on the nation, Koreans maintain a strong sense of nationalism by fiercely holding on to their cultural inheritance.

Aside from celebrating holidays such as National Foundation Day and Independence Movement Day, the present South Korean government also emphasizes the importance of preserving Korea's treasures. A list of historical and cultural relics designates over a thousand items as "Cultural Assets" or "National

Opposite: **Young Koreans may favor modern electronic games, but on special occasions, many of them still enjoy simple traditional games.**

Treasures." These items include the exquisite Korean celadon pottery, the colorful mask dance dramas, and the numerous palaces in Seoul. By drawing on the best of Chinese, Japanese, and Mongolian cultures, Koreans have forged a unique cultural identity for themselves.

On the social and political front, Koreans are not afraid to air their views, although some of their peaceful demonstrations turn violent at times. Nonetheless, the authorities continue to encourage and teach young Koreans — through education — the importance of nation building and constructive criticism.

Above: **These musicians are playing traditional Korean songs. Their costumes resemble those worn by the royal minstrels who performed for the king and his court many years ago.**

1988 Olympics

On September 30, 1981, South Koreans learned that they had been chosen to host the 1988 Summer Olympic Games. Children who were born on that September day were invited to participate in the 1988 opening ceremony in Seoul.

In preparation for the Olympics, the Seoul Olympic Organizing Committee commissioned the building of an Olympic Stadium that could seat 100,000 people. They also built an enormous press center to accommodate the media personnel who would broadcast news of Olympic events around the world.

The Event

The official slogan for the Seoul Olympics was "Peace, Harmony and Progress." While Koreans sought to showcase the wonders of Korean culture, they also wanted to enhance the nation's reputation as an international power. The Olympics, which is televised to millions of viewers around the world, was a perfect opportunity for Korea to step into the spotlight. South Korea dazzled the world with its athletic prowess in a variety of events. The country won twelve gold, ten silver, and eleven bronze

INITIAL PLANS

North and South Korean officials hoped that the peninsula could co-host the Olympics, holding some events in Seoul and some in P'yongyang (the capital of North Korea). In November 1987, however, North Korean agents planted a bomb on a South Korean airliner, killing its 115 passengers. Talks on co-hosting the Olympics became strained and eventually broke down.

Below: Colorful contingents fill the Olympic Stadium in Seoul during the opening ceremony.

Left: During the Olympics, various Korean cultural performances were held, including this lion dance, which is traditionally used to drive away evil spirits.

SOUTH KOREA'S CONTRIBUTION

With each Olympic Games, the host nation is allowed to add a new sport to the list of events. The Seoul Olympic Committee chose to showcase taekwondo. The taekwondo demonstrations were met with much excitement, and taekwondo became an official Olympic sport at the 2000 Games held in Sydney, Australia.

medals, ranking fourth overall, behind the Soviet Union, East Germany (now part of Germany), and the United States. Only 35 of the 160 participating countries medaled in any event.

Diplomatic Triumph

Only North Korea, Cuba, and Ethiopia boycotted the event, making this 24th Olympiad the most attended Olympic Games ever. It was the first time since 1976 that both the Soviet Union and the United States had competed at the same games. This was truly a diplomatic triumph that was largely brought about by Korea's aggressive efforts to promote closer ties with China and the Soviet bloc nations.

Olympic Park

Olympic Park is now a tourist attraction that houses the Seoul Olympic Museum. The museum exhibits over fourteen hundred pieces of memorabilia from the games and an outdoor sculpture garden with Korean and foreign works. Many South Koreans go to the numerous sporting facilities in the Olympic Park to exercise. The stadiums are also used as venues for concerts.

Below: One of the mascots of the 1988 Seoul Olympics was a friendly male tiger named Hodori (*below*). Its female counterpart was named Hosuni. Tigers are well-loved creatures in Korean folklore.

Celadon Pottery

When Buddhism flourished during the Koryo dynasty, Chinese ideas on culture and art were widely received in Korea. One such cultural influence was that of ceramic arts. A group of potters on the Shantung peninsula in China originated the use of blue-green glaze on their pots, known as celadon pottery. Around the year 1050, Korean potters introduced their own innovations to the Chinese techniques.

Celadon pottery production declined at the beginning of the thirteenth century when Korea was subject to numerous Mongol invasions. These invasions disrupted daily life for the Koreans, and the craft of pottery making was subsequently lost. In 1905, the remains of Korean celadon were excavated and brought to light. In addition, archaeologists have found what they believe to be remains of ancient kiln sites in southwestern Korea in what are now the Cholla provinces.

Left: **A potter carves an intricate pattern on this vase, which will then be fired in a kiln.**

Left: **Often tiny little lines are visible below the surface of celadon pottery, which some people mistake for cracks. In fact, the lines are intentional and add to the glaze's beauty.**

Beautiful and Useful Objects

Celadon pottery usually comes in rich green hues. The colors come from minerals in the paint or glaze used to decorate the pots before they are fired in a kiln. The glaze used is rich in iron, which turns green or blue in the kiln. Korean celadon pottery tends to be more lightly glazed than Chinese celadon pottery, allowing some of the clay's natural grayness to shine through. Experts can detect at least sixty different variations in shade and color; the most prized shade is called "kingfisher."

In the past, celadon pottery had a variety of everyday uses, ranging from bowls and plates to decorative vases and incense burners. Celadon designs were fairly plain until around 1150, when elaborate inlaid designs became popular. To make an inlaid design, the artist carved a pattern into the pot before it was fired and filled the carving with white or iron-rich clay. When fired, the etched designs turned white or black, setting them off dramatically from the rest of the pot. Koreans were the first people in the world to use this technique. Today, in the Cholla provinces, an industry devoted to creating replicas of the old styles has taken root.

Cheju

Cheju island, also known as Chejudo, is famous for its aqua-blue beaches, rich foliage, and tropical summer climate. The weather is warmer and rainier than the weather on the mainland, and some of the world's longest lava tubes — the Snake and Manjang caverns — can be found on the island. The capital of the island province is Cheju city, located along the northern shore. Cheju also has its own dialect, which is subtly different from the Korean spoken on the mainland. Shamanism has a strong presence on Cheju, and both male and female shamans still practice today.

The major industries on Cheju are farming, fishing, and tourism. In 2002, President Kim Dae Jung signed a special act to develop Cheju into an international "free" city that allows the free flow of trade and tourism into the island over the next ten years.

Historically, the island was so remote that mainland Koreans did not pay it much heed. Cheju first came under Korean control

Below: **Mount Halla — the highest peak in South Korea — is located on Cheju. The island is a preferred destination for Korean honeymooners, who come to enjoy its tropical weather and breathtaking scenery.**

Left: The haenyo, who range in age from young girls to grandmothers, dive into the ocean to gather seaweed, octopuses, and sea urchins.

during the Koryo era and was given a name that translated as "that place way over there." Around A.D. 900, Cheju became part of the Korean nation. Western explorers first encountered Cheju in 1653, when a group of Dutch sailors on board the *Sparrow Hawk* was shipwrecked on the island. One of the surviving sailors, Hendrik Hamel, wrote a book about his experiences living on the Korean island. Today, the Hamel Monument marks the arrival of Cheju's first European visitors.

Haenyo

Unlike the rest of Asia, a strong matriarchal society developed on Cheju, in which women provided for their families while men stayed at home. Cheju is home to a group of female divers known as *haenyo* (hen-yo). The tradition of women diving goes back over fifteen hundred years and is passed from mother to daughter. Because women have more layers of fat than men, they are better equipped to withstand the icy waters off the Cheju coast. Although they now don wet suits, the haenyo do not use any scuba gear. They dive as deep as 60 feet (18 m) under water, holding their breath for three to five minutes at a time. The women dive for hours during the summer — up to 150 times a day — and even brave winter temperatures, which can drop to 50° F (10° C). The number of haenyo is dwindling because most women now choose less physically demanding jobs.

Below: Shaped as wise old men, *Harubang* (hah-roo-bong) can be found throughout Cheju. Anthropologists are unsure what purpose these statues once served.

Computer Chips and Cyber Games

As one of the "Four Dragons of East Asia," South Korea boasts a strong manufacturing industry that produces a wide range of high-tech products, including computers, digital versatile disks (DVDs), and telecommunications equipment. The nation is one of the largest producers of silicon chips, or microchips, in the world and, in recent years, has emerged at the forefront of the Internet and cyber games.

Top Korean Electronics Manufacturers

Samsung Electronics Company Limited is one of the world's leading manufacturers of microchips. The company is also one of the top mobile telephone manufacturers in the world, ranking fourth in terms of sales. Samsung makes many other products, including portable computers, desktop computers, fax machines, televisions, and camcorders. These products helped make Samsung one of the top fifty most recognizable brands in the world in 2001.

MICROCHIPS AND APPLIANCES

Microchips, more commonly known as chips, are tiny pieces of material made from elements such as silicon or germanium. These chips conduct electricity. When fitted with tiny electronic devices, the chips help power a wide range of electrical appliances and electronic equipment that are used in everyday life. Chips can be found in computers, credit cards, mobile telephones, and washing machines, among other things.

Left: The woman on the left demonstrates the use of a credit card that has been embedded with a microchip. When connected to a mobile telephone, this credit card allows users to make online purchases. Some South Korean mobile telephone network companies offer this innovative credit card.

LG Electronics is another internationally famous South Korean company, known for its many electrical appliances, such as air conditioners, washing machines, and flat screen televisions. LG Electronics' air conditioners are sold in more than one hundred countries around the world, and LG Electronics factories worldwide produce millions of air conditioning units each year.

Cyber Games

South Korea is one of the leading Internet nations in the world. Approximately half of the country's homes are connected to the "information superhighway." South Koreans love to surf the Internet, shop online, and play online games. In fact, playing cyber games is the latest phenomenon to hit South Korea.

Online gaming, or playing cyber games, on personal computers is more popular in South Korea than the home video consoles that are preferred in most other countries. The popularity of the games is mainly due to the rapid spread of broadband, which is needed to fully enjoy graphics-intensive Internet games. As a result, online games are now one of the nation's fastest growing industries, and the country has quickly become the online games capital of the world.

South Koreans excel at cyber games. Today, around 65 percent of all Korean Internet surfers visit online game sites, and the country boasts five million active Internet "gamers" who play online games.

The DMZ and Panmunjom

At the Cairo Conference in 1943, Great Britain, the United States, and China agreed that Korea would be an independent nation "in due course." In the meantime, a secret treaty was signed at Yalta stating that the Soviet Union would gain control of the northern part of the Korean peninsula if it assisted the three powers in defeating Japan. At the end of the war, the Japanese were defeated, and the 38th parallel of latitude became the dividing line between North Korea and South Korea. This division became even more indelible when the Demilitarized Zone, or DMZ, was determined at the cease-fire of the Korean War in 1953. Since the collapse of the Soviet Union, the DMZ stands as one of the lasting remnants of Cold War international politics.

Technically, the Korean War has never ended; the two sides have simply observed an extended cease-fire. Panmunjom, a village located along the DMZ, has been witness to the ongoing

Below: **Falling roughly along the 38th parallel, the DMZ is strip of land 2.5 miles (4 km) wide that runs for 155 miles (249 km), separating the peninsula. Down the center of the strip, 1,292 white markers hold signs indicating the physical dividing line known as the Military Demarcation Line (MDL). A barbed-wire fence guarded with outposts and military personnel runs alongside the MDL.**

North Korean-South Korean conflict. On July 27, 1953, the Korean Armistice Agreement was signed following the longest truce talks in history. Panmunjom, which is also known as the Joint Security Area (JSA), has been the site of further negotiations between North Korean and South Korean officials, although a formal peace treaty has yet to be signed.

In 1972, Red Cross talks commenced in Panmunjom with the goal of reunifying the two countries. In 1974, however, four infiltration tunnels were discovered under the DMZ, presumably built to aid a North Korean invasion. Since then, the area immediately south of the DMZ has been heavily militarized. Now that North Korea has hinted at nuclear capacities, the world is even more eager for the two countries to reach an agreeable and long-term settlement.

Wildlife in the DMZ

Since no one is allowed within the DMZ, the area has become a wildlife sanctuary for endangered plants and animals such as Asiatic black bears, white-naped and red-crowned cranes, and Amur leopards. Many birds stop at the DMZ as part of their regular migratory patterns. Scientists from all over the world study the different species that live in peace there.

Above: **A meeting between North Korean and South Korean officials, regarding reunification of the peninsula, was held by the Red Cross in 1984 at Panmunjom.**

BROKEN FAMILIES

During World War II and the Korean War, many families attempted to flee south (and some north) but were prevented by the construction of the border. Limited visits between relatives have taken place as part of political maneuvering between the two countries, and the majority of Koreans hope that the day of reunification will soon arrive.

Ginseng

Ginseng is one of the most prominent herbs in traditional Oriental medicine, and ancient Koreans even believed it was the elixir of life. Ginseng is native to the Korean forests and is perhaps Korea's oldest and most famous export product. Korean records indicate that ginseng was shipped to China and Japan over 1,500 years ago. During the Koryo dynasty, Koreans paid tribute to the Chinese emperor with offerings of ginseng. In Korea, ginseng is known as *insam* (in-sum).

Although once widespread throughout the peninsula, ginseng was overharvested and became rather scarce about one thousand years ago. Today, the Korean government strictly regulates the ginseng market. The best ginseng is grown in soil made of decayed chestnut and oak leaves and takes from four to six years to come to full maturity. Good cultivation areas for ginseng are rare, making high-quality ginseng very expensive.

Below: **Farmers build straw roofs over their ginseng plants to shade and protect them. Ginseng roots are harvested by hand with a two-pronged tool and then steamed or dried.**

Left: Sliced or whole ginseng roots are often soaked in tea or liquor, and this liquid is used as a tonic. Bottled tonics can be easily found in South Korea.

Red and White Ginseng

Ginseng roots are specially processed to make either white or red ginseng. Red ginseng is produced by a long, careful steaming process that causes the ginseng to become slightly pink. Because red ginseng is more potent, it is more suitable for the elderly or the sick. The Korean government closely monitors the amount of red ginseng that leaves the country through export. White ginseng is relatively inexpensive and widely available. Ginseng roots are classified according to size and quality. Lesser-quality roots may be ground into extracts for tea or medicine.

Ginseng for Overall Well-Being

In the past, ginseng was thought to be an all-purpose medicine for a variety of illnesses, ranging from a toothache to epilepsy. Even today, Koreans tend to take ginseng for any kind of medical disorder, although its benefits have not been fully proven.

Today, many scientists believe ginseng stimulates the nervous system, if taken in small amounts. Research also indicates that ginseng is rich in essential vitamins and minerals. Many herbal beverages on the market today contain extracts of ginseng that are supposed to improve mental clarity. Ginseng is also made into tablets or capsules for medicinal purposes. The most common way to consume ginseng is to steep it in tea.

"POWER" BEVERAGE

Koreans make a traditional drink consisting of ginseng root, dried jujubes, and pine nuts, which are boiled together with a little sugar. This drink can be prepared at home or purchased at ginseng teahouses. Ginseng teahouses are popular throughout Korea and can be identified by a picture of a ginseng root on the door.

Hanbok: Traditional Costume

Most modern Koreans dress as high fashion dictates, wearing the styles seen on television or in magazines. The Koreans on the streets of Seoul dress just like Canadians in Ottawa or Americans in Washington, D.C. Older Koreans or those living in rural areas, though, may wear the traditional Korean clothing known as *hanbok* (hahn-bock).

The hanbok for Korean men includes a loose jacket, called a *chogori* (cho-gore-ee), and baggy pants gathered at the ankles, called *paji* (pah-jee). The traditional hat worn with a hanbok is tall, black, and stove pipe-shaped, usually with a wide brim and a long silk cord. Known as a *kat* (cot), this style of hat was developed during the Silla period and did not go out of fashion until the twentieth

Left: **An elderly man dons his hanbok, with traditional shoes and hat.**

HANBOK'S MIXED HERITAGE

The hanbok of today evolved from a mixture of Chinese and Mongol styles. By the fifteenth century, the women's hanbok style settled into the high-waisted flowing design seen today. For both men and women, the hanbok jacket has been shorter or longer, according to prevailing fashion trends.

century. Both men and women carry their money or belongings in a small pouch, since traditional Korean clothing has no pockets.

A Korean woman's hanbok is usually a long, full, high-waisted wraparound skirt known as a *chima* (chee-mah). The woman's chogori, a short blouse with long, full sleeves that ties in the front, is worn over the chima. The sash of the blouse is tied in an elaborate knot, with the ends hanging decoratively over the ensemble. A well-made hanbok has a neat collar, elegantly shaped sleeves, and a one-sided bow.

Hanboks are tailormade to fit both the age and social status of the wearer, as well as the occasion for which the ensemble is being made. Colorful hanboks with elaborately striped sleeves are commonly worn by children. Young girls wear bright red skirts and yellow jackets with striped sleeves, but when they grow older they may choose more sedate colors. White is a popular color for women because it is cool in the summer. Men rarely wear white hanboks until they are elderly, signifying that they no longer work. Summer hanboks may be made of light silks, while those worn in winter may be made from heavy silk brocades or satins. Clothing designed for everyday wear is made of cotton or linen.

Above: **A woman's hanbok is loose fitting, and the cloth is so voluminous that her figure is concealed.**

Hangul and King Sejong

King Sejong (r. 1418 –1450), the fourth king of the Yi dynasty, was known throughout his kingdom as a highly educated man who patronized science and the arts. The best scholars in the country came to court to study with him and to work with like-minded intellectuals. When King Sejong had an idea, the best minds in the land were close at hand to help him implement it.

Before the invention of hangul, Koreans used Chinese characters to express their thoughts in writing. Not all Koreans, however, were able to read Chinese because this involved memorizing thousands of Chinese characters just to achieve basic literacy. Since Confucian thought was the backbone of Korean society, King Sejong felt that every Korean should be able to read its texts. To fulfill his wish of creating a common written language, King Sejong commissioned linguists to study how Koreans talked. Based on their study, the linguists devised a phonetic alphabet that corresponded to common sounds. King Sejong presented the resulting hangul alphabet to his court at the end of 1446.

HANGUL AND ENGLISH

Sometimes Korean words are hard to write in English. For example, the Korean language does not make a distinction between the two sounds for B and P, and there is only one Korean letter for both L and R. Thus, a Korean word may be written in several different ways in English.

Left: After the creation of hangul, many important Confucianist and Buddhist texts were translated into hangul so that more people could read them. The Haeinsa temple (*left*) in Taegu houses the Tripitaka Koreana, a set of 81,258 wooden blocks containing carved Buddhist scriptures. The blocks were completed in the thirteenth century.

Despite King Sejong's strong interest in promoting the new written language, hangul met with strong resistance from some members of his court. The use of hangul, scholars argued, removed the Chinese classics from their contexts. Later, when Christian missionaries came to Korea, they used hangul translations of the Bible to spread Christianity among the Korean people. Hangul then began to gain more prominence as the common written language.

Hangul has changed little since King Sejong's time. The twenty-four letters in the Korean alphabet consist of ten vowels and fourteen consonants. Characters are combinations of these consonants and vowels.

Hangul's close relationship to actual speech made reading very easy to learn, and Korea soon had one of the highest literacy rates in the world. Koreans celebrate Hangul Day on October 9.

Kim Dae Jung: Prisoner to President

Kim Dae Jung was born on December 3, 1925, on a small island called Hauido off the southwestern Korean coast. After graduating from high school, Kim ran a Japanese shipping company that was left in his hands when Japan lost control of Korea. He continued to run the shipping company during the Korean War, even after escaping North Korean imprisonment.

During the 1950s, Kim launched his political career. After losing several National Assembly bids, he finally won a seat in 1961. He was reelected and served in the Assembly until 1971, when he ran for president against the dictator Park Chung Hee. Park's supporters were shocked when Kim nearly won the bid for president during this election.

Left: **Kim Dae Jung speaks at a political rally in Seoul before his arrest in 1974.**

Left: **During the 1980s, several international groups nominated Kim Dae Jung for the Nobel Peace Prize, naming him a champion of human rights and democracy. In October 2000, the Nobel Committee in Oslo, Norway, awarded Kim the Nobel Peace Prize from a record field of 150 nominees.**

Kim's life took a turn for the worse when he became Park's political rival. In 1971, Kim was in a car accident; a truck rammed his vehicle, killing his driver and leaving Kim with a permanent limp. Then, in 1973, he was kidnapped by South Korean intelligence when receiving medical treatment in Tokyo, Japan, and later almost drowned at sea. After this incident, Kim was placed under house arrest and then jailed. He was not released until Park was assassinated in 1979. When Chun Doo Hwan came into power in 1980, he sentenced Kim to death for inciting the Kwangju uprising that year. Kim was only spared when U.S. president Ronald Reagan intervened. Kim was then exiled to the United States. He did not return to South Korea until 1985.

After losing to Kim Young Sam in the 1992 presidential election, Kim Dae Jung finally won the presidency in 1997 and was inaugurated in early 1998. At that time, South Korea was in financial crisis, and much of Kim's energy was devoted to easing the country's economic problems.

In 2000, Kim grabbed the world's attention when he successfully engineered the first inter-Korean summit since the Korean peninsula's political division. During a three-day meeting held in June, Kim Dae Jung met his North Korean counterpart, Kim Jong-il, and the two leaders devised a five-point joint declaration about the future of the Korean peninsula.

Kimchi: A Savory Staple

At almost every meal in a Korean household, at least two dishes will be served: kimchi and rice, to cool down kimchi's hot flavor. Kimchi is the national dish of South Korea.

Kimchi is a highly seasoned, pickled salad made from a combination of vegetables and spices. More than 150 kinds of kimchi are documented — a museum in Seoul displays over one hundred versions — and the most common kind is *napa* (nah-pah) kimchi, which is made with Chinese cabbage. Turnips, radishes, cucumbers, and even salted fish or shrimp are sometimes added. Kimchi gets its characteristically sharp and spicy flavor through the process of pickling. The seasonings used are usually a combination of garlic, ginger, red pepper, scallions, and salt.

Below: To the uninitiated, all kimchi may taste "hot." In fact, kimchi can range from mild to spicy, depending on the spices used and length of pickling. In warmer climates, more seasoning and pickling are necessary to preserve the vegetables for longer periods; therefore, kimchi made in the southern parts of the peninsula is spicier.

Left: **Traditionally, kimchi is placed in large earthen jars and buried underground or placed somewhere cool and dark to ferment for weeks.**

A Healthy Dish

The ingredients of kimchi are pickled with salt, and this process produces lactic acid. Like the bacteria found in yogurt, this lactic acid aids digestion and is beneficial for the stomach and intestines. Kimchi is also high in fiber and vitamins and low in fat, which makes the dish a healthy diet choice.

Kimchi All Year Round

Traditionally, women made large batches of kimchi during the tenth month of the lunar calendar, usually late October or early November. This period of preparation was known as *kimjang* (kim-jon). Making kimchi was an intuitive and inherited knowledge passed down through the generations. Married women learned how to make kimchi from their mothers-in-law; thus, each family's kimchi had its own history and distinct flavor.

Today, Koreans have less time to prepare batches of kimchi. Many varieties are available ready-made in stores. For women who prefer to make their own kimchi, special refrigerators are specifically designed for storing and pickling, or fermenting, small batches of kimchi.

As intercultural exchange among the world's nations increases, kimchi has found a place in international cuisine. Once a simple side dish or a quick component of leftovers, kimchi is now turning up in burgers and on pizzas.

Kwangju Massacre

In 1961, Park Chung Hee took control of the South Korean government after staging a military coup. He then increased the power of the military and limited democratic reforms. Because his policies were so unpopular, Park was assassinated in 1979. He was succeeded, however, by an equally militant successor, General Chun Doo Hwan, in 1980.

When school resumed in March 1980, students protested against Chun's government. They demanded that the government relax its strict laws, particularly the martial law that limited human rights and freedom of speech. They also did not want Chun to be in charge because he was a remnant of Park's oppressive regime.

In May 1980, Chun Doo Hwan closed down all colleges and universities and prohibited civilian political gatherings. All publications and broadcasts were censored, criticism of past and current governments was forbidden, and the manufacture and spreading of rumors became a crime. By imposing these highly restrictive laws, Chun caused great outrage among the South Korean students.

Below: **Students gather in Kwangju to protest Chun's regime.**

Left: **This grave of a young student who died during the protests in Kwangju is located in Mangwol Cemetery. The cemetery was established in Kwangju in memory of people who died during the protests.**

Below: **After the revolt, General Chun Doo Hwan toured Kwangju and told residents not to make an issue of what happened but to learn from the tragedy. The uprising marked the beginning of anti-American sentiments in South Korea, as some U.S. troops had helped quell the riots and U.S. president Ronald Reagan had endorsed Chun's policies.**

This standoff came to a climax in Kwangju, a city of 600,000 people located in the South Cholla Province. The uprising and bloodbath that occurred between May 18 and May 27 are known as the Kwangju massacre. Although not as well-known as the 1989 Tiananmen Square uprising in Beijing, China, the Kwangju massacre was equally devastating in scope.

On May 18, students began demonstrating against the new military edicts limiting their rights. Rumors spread that soldiers had been sent to eliminate the people of South Cholla Province, so many citizens joined the students in the streets. Special Forces units broke up the demonstration, killing large numbers of people. Riots and further demonstrations occurred over the next week. On May 27, an army division launched an attack on the Kwangju students and citizens. After light skirmishes, the army quashed the revolt in less than two hours. Official counts say about two hundred people died, but Kwangju residents place the death toll closer to two thousand.

In 1996, the South Korean court sentenced Chun Doo Hwan to death, largely due to his role in ordering the Kwangju massacre. However, President Kim Dae Jung pardoned Chun in 1997.

Legend of Tangun

The legend of Tangun is famous among both North and South Koreans. It describes the founding of ancient Korea. According to the legend, more than four thousand years ago, a bear and a tiger yearned to become human. They prayed for the divine creator Hwanin to transform them into human beings. Hwanin's son, Hwanung, heard their prayers and came to Earth to meet them. Hwanung appeared by a sandalwood tree in the Taebaek Mountains and became the ruler of the Korean peninsula.

Taking the title of *Chonwang* (chong-wang), which means "King of Heaven," Hwanung received three thousand followers. From his followers, Hwanung selected ministers to tend to the weather and to teach the people the secrets of art, science, culture, and ethics.

When Hwanung met the bear and tiger, he gave them instructions on how to achieve human form. The two animals had to consume bitter mugwort and garlic and stay out of the sun for one hundred days in order to turn into humans. The bear and tiger ate the herbs and then went and stayed in a dark cave. The tiger was impatient and left too soon, so it never became a human.

Left: **The myth of the bear-god (Tangun) is a common theme in many folk religions. The bear-woman (Ungnyo) is often believed to come from a bear totem tribe, or a tribe that is symbolized by the bear.**

Left: **Mount Mani, on Kanghwa island, stands at 1,536 ft (468 m).**

The bear, however, followed Hwanung's instructions and turned into a beautiful woman named Ungnyo.

As a woman, Ungnyo's greatest wish was to have a child. Therefore, she went to the sandalwood tree where Hwanung had first appeared on the peninsula and prayed that she might bear a child. Hearing her prayers, Hwanung temporarily turned himself into a man, and they had a son. When Ungnyo's son was born in 2333 B.C., she named him Tangun Wanggom, which means "Sandalwood King."

Tangun became the first human king of Korea. He named his domain Choson ("Land of Morning Calm"), established his capital in present-day P'yongyang, and ruled for twelve hundred years. The era of his rule is known as Ancient Choson. Tangun taught the inhabitants how to farm and care for animals. He also built a huge altar on Mount Mani, a mountain on Kanghwa island off the western coast of Korea. In 1122 B.C., Tangun abdicated and became a mountain god.

A religious cult, called *Taejonggyo* (tie-jahng-gee-oh), then developed around the worship of Tangun. The faith, however, mostly died out during the fifteenth century. In recent years, interest in the Tangun myth was renewed, and a few sects have now revived the religion.

"REMAINS" OF THE ANCIENT ALTAR

Interestingly, remains of an ancient altar at the summit of Mount Mani on Kanghwa island have been discovered. Although most people do not accept the legend as historical fact, the South Korean government has designated the altar remains as an official National Treasure.

Mask Dances

Mask dance dramas developed during the early days of the Choson Dynasty. Today, three common themes can be found in mask dramas: ridiculing monks who bother young women; making fun of the upper class known as the *yangban* (yahng-bahn); and dramatizing conflicts between husbands and their wives and concubines or second wives. By wearing masks, dancers have been able to anonymously pinpoint society's faults.

Above: **Black cloth is often attached to the back of masks. This cloth helps the wearers keep the masks on. The cloth also looks like black hair.**

Left: **Masks are commonly made of wood, gourds, or papier-mâché. Papier-mâché and gourd masks are very popular because the materials are lightweight and easy to find. Masks are usually made from one piece of material, although some masks have movable eyeballs and chins, which allow a greater range of expression.**

The expressions on the masks are greatly exaggerated because mask dances were traditionally performed at night by dim firelight. Bright and striking colors are used for the same reason. Black masks symbolize old people, red masks represent young men, and white masks symbolize young women. This color code enables viewers of mask dramas to instantly recognize the characters, even if they do not know the story.

In the past, making masks was not considered an art in Korea, so little is known about the craftsmen who made them. Both the artists and the dancers who performed in the dramas belonged to the lowest class of entertainers. Few old masks exist today because masks were often burned at the end of dramatic performances or religious rites. Both artistic and religious masks became "contaminated" during exposure to the spirit world and had to be destroyed to avoid bad luck.

The Korean government has designated several mask dances as "Intangible Cultural Assets" so future generations may study and enjoy them. One of these, the Hahoe mask dance, is over five hundred years old and is still performed in the village of Hahoe near Andong in North Kyongsang.

Above: **By using animated body gestures, dancers can express a wide range of emotions, even while wearing masks. Dialogue is almost nonexistent in the dramas. Instead, music and dance are used to tell the story.**

RELIGIOUS AND ARTISTIC MASKS

Korean masks date back to prehistoric times and fall under two main categories: religious and artistic. Religious masks evolved out of shamanistic rites and are often worn to frighten off evil spirits. Used essentially in dramas, artistic masks also have a certain degree of religious function.

Seoul

Seoul, a capital city since the Choson dynasty, is rich in history but is also modern and streamlined. The citizens of Seoul are employed in government, technology, and service sectors. The country's major banks and industrial corporations, such as Hyundai and Samsung, are headquartered in Seoul. All major government offices as well as the best universities are also located in the capital. Many international conventions are held in Seoul because of its central location. On the streets of Seoul, young people often carry cell phones, listen to popular music, and enjoy many different types of cuisine. Almost a quarter of the nation's population lives in Seoul, as it is the political, economic, and educational hub of the country.

Left: **The streets of Seoul are often swamped with people, and the sidewalks are lined with numerous shops and restaurants.**

Remains of the Korean Monarchy

Some of the most popular attractions in Seoul are the remains of four palaces dating from the Yi dynasty. The largest is Kyongbok Palace, built in 1394. The palace contains numerous buildings, including Sujongjon, or the Hall of Talented Scholars. This hall was where hangul was invented during King Sejong's reign. Another magnificent structure is a ten-story pagoda that dates back to the Koryo era, over six hundred years ago.

Changdok Palace, which means "Palace of Illustrious Virtue," was built in 1405 as an extension of Kyongbok. The palace was destroyed by Japanese invaders in 1592 and rebuilt by 1611. Choson royalty lived in Changdok Palace, including Princess Yi Pang-ja, the last surviving member of the royal family who died in 1989. The royal garage still houses the first car in Korea — a 1903 Cadillac owned by King Sunjong. Behind Changdok is Piwon, the royal family's Secret Garden.

Changgyong Palace was a summer residence that once contained a zoo. Toksu Palace is the most recently built palace in Seoul. King Kojong (r. 1897–1910), the penultimate king of the Yi dynasty, lived out his final days here.

Above: **The Hyangwonjong Pavilion of Kyongbok Palace provides a scenic view for visitors.**

Taekwondo: A Traditional Martial Art

Taekwondo, which means "the way of feet and fists," is one of the most popular martial arts in the world today. This challenging art form involves using complicated physical maneuvers.

Beginnings

The origins of taekwondo date back more than two thousand years. The knights of the Korean military developed a style of fighting that used bare hands and feet instead of weapons. These knights, known as the *hwarangdo* (hwah-rang-doh), flourished during the Silla dynasty. The hwarangdo were roughly equivalent to the samurai warrior class in Japan. Two of the oldest existing records of Korean history — the *Samguk sagi* and the *Samguk yusa* — indicate that the hwarangdo used taekwondo exercises in their basic training.

Left: Taekwondo demonstrations often involve breaking planks of wood in spectacular displays of physical prowess.

Left: **In a daeryun, taekwondo students learn the finer points of using their strength and speed.**

Forms and Breaks

A competition, or *daeryun* (die-ryoung), allows taekwondo students to practice their fighting techniques in a pseudo-military setting. For practice or demonstration, both participants follow a prearranged sequence of attacks. In freestyle competitions, the competitors use any of their taekwondo techniques to attack or defend themselves as needed.

Apart from a daeryun, the two other basic components of taekwondo training are form, or *hyung* (he-young), and breaking, or *kyukpa* (kee-yuk-pah). Forms are stylized sequences of attacks that demonstrate varying degrees of difficulty. An individual form consists of twenty to fifty stances, each of which involves either an attack, a blocking move, or a combination of both. In breaking tests, participants practice hitting and kicking blocks of wood or other objects to demonstrate their acquired powers without harming another person.

Proficiency Levels

Colored belts, worn with the taekwondo uniforms, indicate the wearer's level of proficiency. A white belt means a student is a beginner, while experienced students may acquire many degrees of black belts. For taekwondo students to progress through the levels, they must demonstrate a knowledge of martial arts philosophy, a proper attitude toward the art, and increasingly advanced technical skills.

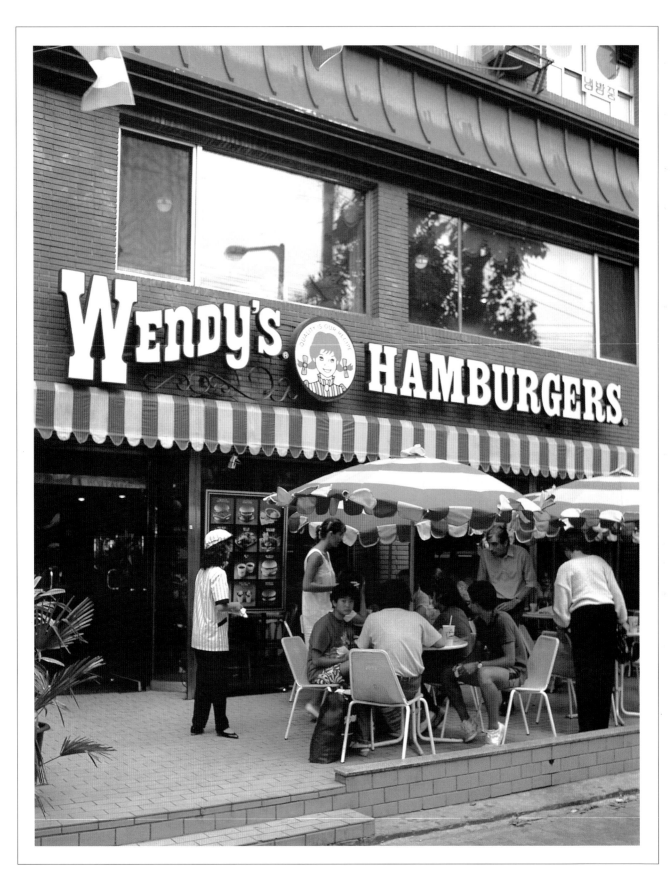

74

RELATIONS WITH NORTH AMERICA

South Korea's relationship with North America has been relatively intense. Because of Korea's historically isolationist position, Americans did not enter the country until the nineteenth century. Since then, North America has played a large role in Korean history, both in the political and cultural arenas.

Americans living in South Korea are most visible in the armed forces. Since the Korean War, the United States has maintained troops in South Korea, especially along the Demilitarized Zone. The American presence is aimed at preventing any future invasion by North Korea. After the

Below: **On March 7, 2001, U.S. president George W. Bush met with South Korea's President Kim Dae Jung in the Oval Office at the White House in Washington, D.C.**

Kwangju massacre in 1980, when U.S. troops were used to help end the demonstrations, the South Korean people have been increasingly unhappy with what they perceive as American interference in their country's politics.

Korean immigrants to various parts of North America have been instrumental in shaping the landscape of North American culture. Koreans have been active in the labor force since they first arrived on the continent, bringing with them professional skills and a strong work ethic. Christian communities in North America have also gained large following of Koreans.

Opposite: **In South Korea, American fast food is a popular alternative to Korean cuisine.**

Early Encounters

In the past, Koreans were unwilling to welcome foreigners from the West into their country. In 1866, the U.S. trading ship *General Sherman* attempted to make contact with the Korean people, but the ship was set afire by local residents and soldiers, killing everyone on board. In 1871, U.S. naval vessels were also turned away. Americans were finally allowed to enter Korea when the United States and Korea signed the Treaty of Amity and Commerce in 1882.

Lucius H. Foote became the first U.S. minister to Korea in 1883. Foote served in Seoul as an advisor to the Choson government. Within a year of his arrival, he organized Korea's first diplomatic envoy to the United States. Another early U.S. minister to Korea was Horace N. Allen, a Presbyterian missionary and medical doctor.

Protestant missionaries began arriving in the Korean peninsula in 1884 and 1885. In addition to spreading Christianity, the missionaries brought with them ideas of modern Western education. Paichai Haktang, the first modern boys' school in Korea, was established by American Methodist missionary Henry G. Appenzeller in 1885.

Left: **This illustration shows Korean officials arriving in the United States in 1883.**

Left: **During the Korean War (1950–1953), Korean immigrants in North America did whatever they could to help war victims back home. Some participated in the Korean Clothes Drive, donating clothing which was sent to Korea.**

The Journey to the United States

At the beginning of the twentieth century, many Hawaiian sugar plantations recruited Asian immigrants to work on the Hawaiian islands. The first big wave of Korean immigration to America occurred when a group of one hundred Korean laborers arrived in Hawaii in 1903. Thousands followed over the next three years; among them were Christian converts who believed they could practice their religion more freely in a Christian country. The sugar plantation laborers faced hard working conditions. They worked long hours (ten-hour days) in the hot fields, six days a week. Workers were banned from joining unions. Women had to do as much work as the men but for less pay. Most of these immigrants soon moved to the west coast of the United States.

When Korea came under Japanese control after Japan defeated Russia in 1905, Japan stopped Korean immigration to Hawaii. In 1907, Japan and the United States made a "gentlemen's agreement," which limited Japanese immigration to the United States. Since Korea was under Japanese rule, this agreement limited Korean immigration as well. The only Koreans allowed to enter the United States were wives of Korean men already living in the country. In 1924, Korean immigration halted completely when the United States passed the Immigration Act, prohibiting all Asians from entering the country. This act was later repealed.

Korean Immigration after the Korean War

A second large wave of Korean immigration occurred after the Korean War. Many American soldiers stationed in Korea during the war met and married Korean women. Even after the war, intermarriage occurred between Korean women and American men stationed at Korean bases. When the soldiers returned to their homeland, they took their wives with them. Between 1951 and 1964, over twenty-eight thousand Korean women emigrated to the United States as soldiers' wives.

In 1965, the Hart-Cellar Act was passed, allowing twenty thousand immigrants per Eastern Hemisphere country per year to enter the United States. This act led to the third great wave of immigration. The act also favored educated immigrants, so many professionals chose to move to the United States.

KOREANS IN CANADIAN CITIES

Annually, more that nine thousand Koreans emigrate to Canada. The 140,000 Korean immigrants living in Canada today often settle down in Toronto, Vancouver, and Ottawa.

Left: **Since 1975, Korea has been one of the top five countries of origin for immigrants to the United States. Today, California and New York have the greatest populations of Korean immigrants. A Koreatown (*left*) has been established in Los Angeles, California, which is home to the largest population of Koreans outside Seoul.**

Left: **This photo shows the extended families of two adopted Korean children. All of them are currently living in the United States.**

Korean Orphans

Beginning in the 1950s, another group of Koreans began making their way into North America: orphaned children. Some of these children lost their families in the Korean War that ended in 1953. Since Korean families believed strongly in blood lineage, adoption was not favored in Korea. Therefore, the orphaned children were put up for foreign adoption.

Korean adoption was extremely popular in North America, especially in the 1980s. Since 1954, over 150,000 Korean children have been adopted by families all over the world, including the United States and Canada. Each year approximately two thousand more children, some with severe birth defects, are adopted internationally. Today, two-thirds of abandoned children in Korea are adopted by foreign families.

Several support groups around the world have been set up for families who have adopted Korean infants. These groups often conduct tours of South Korea so that adoptees can visit their homeland and understand their heritage. Most big cities in North America have organizations where Korean adoptees can meet and share their experiences, such as the Association of Korean Adoptees that meets in San Francisco, California.

Left: U.S. Army General Douglas MacArthur (*left*) and Korea's first president, Syngman Rhee (*right*), converse during ceremonies in Seoul on August 15, 1948. The date marks the inauguration of the government of the Republic of Korea and the third anniversary of Korea's liberation from Japanese rule.

Relations during the Cold War

The United States kept a low profile in Korean politics until World War II in 1939. During the war, the United States sought support from the Soviet Union in the war against Japan. The Soviets gave their support, in exchange for control of northern Korea after the war. The United States consented without informing the Koreans of the agreement. Thus, when Korea was divided after the war, the Soviet Union strongly influenced the north, while the United States influenced the south.

The end of World War II in 1945 marked the beginning of the Cold War during which turbulent relations developed between the United States and the Soviet Union. The U.S. government feared the spread of communism by the Soviets in Asia. Thus, when South Korea held its first elections in 1948, the United States supported presidential candidate Syngman Rhee, for his conservative stance against communist ideas. North Korea responded to the election by severing all ties with both the United States and South Korea and shutting off the electricity supply to South Korea.

Given South Korea's precarious position, the United States was less eager to be involved in South Korea's affairs. In June 1950, however, North Korean forces, with Soviet reinforcements, invaded South Korea, sparking the Korean War. Seeing that the South Korean army was ill-prepared to defend the country, U.S. president Harry S. Truman's administration quickly committed troops to South Korea's defense. U.S. general Douglas MacArthur commanded the landing of United Nations forces — largely composed of North Americans — at Inch'on and turned the tide of the Korean War. China then allied itself with the North Koreans, and neither side could gain an advantage. A cease-fire was signed in 1953, but the United Nations continues to station troops in South Korea to prevent future invasions.

During Park Chung Hee's presidency, South Korea maintained close ties with the United States. South Korea sent troops to aid U.S. forces during the Vietnam War, and President Lyndon B. Johnson visited Seoul in 1966 as a gesture of appreciation. Tensions arose, however, when Jimmy Carter won the presidential election in 1976 and promised to remove U.S. troops from South Korea, which caused a low point in U.S.-South Korean diplomatic relations. Relations improved when President Ronald Reagan, elected in 1980, pledged no further withdrawal of U.S. troops from South Korea.

CANADIANS IN THE KOREAN WAR

Canadian troops fought alongside South Korean soldiers during the Korean War. A total of 26,791 Canadian troops fought in the war, and 516 Canadian soldiers died in battle.

Left: A Korean War veteran visits the United Nations Memorial Cemetery in South Korea.

Living in North America

Before emigrating, many Koreans save money so they can start a business and become self-employed in North America. Over two million Korean-Americans and Korean-Canadians live in North America today.

In the United States, Koreans have the highest rate of self-employment among Asians, which is twice as high as the American average. The most common business for Koreans to start in the United States is a small grocery store. Today, Koreans run more than three quarters of the grocery shops in both Los Angeles and New York City. The stores are usually family-run businesses. Many Korean grocers buy their supplies from Korean distributors so money is circulated within the community. The grocer system results in a close-knit Korean community with few ties to non-Koreans, apart from those who shop in the stores.

Since most Korean immigrants who live in North America are Christians, the number of Korean churches in the United States and Canada has increased. Churches that cater to Korean congregations include the Korean Church of Memphis in Tennessee and the Ottawa Korean Community Church in Canada, which conduct separate services in English and Korean.

Jeanette Lee: Against All Obstacles

Born in Brooklyn, New York, as a first generation Korean-American, Jeanette Lee is one of the world's top pool (billiard) players.

At the age of thirteen, Lee was diagnosed with scoliosis, or a curved spine. To prevent the condition from worsening, doctors implanted a steel rod in her back. Her physical condition, however, did not stop her from pursuing her love for pool, which began at the age of eighteen. Lee practiced for as long as twelve hours a day and read books about the techniques of playing pool. Four years later, she became a professional pool player. Within a year, she was ranked among the top ten pool players in the world. Despite suffering from constant back pain, Lee's grim determination has helped her become one of the top competitors in her sport while winning her countless fans around the world.

Left: Jeanette Lee has won fifteen Women's Professional Billiard Association (WPBA) Classic Tour titles. She was also named "Player of the Year" in 1994 and "Sports Person of the Year" in 1998 by the WPBA.

Living Abroad

North Americans work, travel, and study in South Korea to experience its unique cultural atmosphere and history. Many North American companies have branches in Korea and send their top executives to staff offices in Seoul.

Every year, the best universities in North America, such as McGill University in Canada and the University of California in the United States, send exchange students to study abroad at Yonsei University in Seoul. More than forty Korean and Canadian educational institutions participate in such exchange programs, which promote closer understanding between the students from these countries.

In addition, more than one thousand Canadian English teachers are invited to South Korea each year to teach in the public education system or in private schools. The Ministry of Education and the Provincial Offices of Education in Korea jointly recruit teachers from six major English-speaking nations, including Canada and the United States, through the English Program in Korea (EPIK).

Above: **The University of California is one U.S. university system that offers exchange programs for Korean students.**

U.S. Military Forces in South Korea

Today, about thirty-seven thousand U.S. troops are stationed in South Korea to safeguard the nation against any possible attacks from North Korea. These troops are called the United States Forces in Korea (USFK).

These military forces, however, have had unfortunate run-ins with the local people. In 1980, when U.S. military forces helped end the Kwangju uprising that resulted in civilian deaths, Koreans began to resent the United States. Since then, the Korean public has constantly displayed dissatisfaction with the U.S. military presence. During the mid-1990s, large rallies often took place outside the main USFK headquarters in South Korea to protest crimes committed by American military men.

In 2000, Korean students and environmentalists protested the USFK's dumping of toxic chemicals into the Seoul sewage system without proper treatment. Even though the USFK made a public apology for the dumping, the apology did little to ease the strained relations between the USFK and the Korean students and environmentalists. Incidents like these often create anti-American sentiments among the Korean public.

Left: **These American soldiers (shown wearing ties) are in Panmunjom on the border between North Korea and South Korea.**

CHINA

NORTH
KOREA

*Korea
Bay*

■ P'YONGYANG

*Sea of
Japan*

DMZ

Panmunjom
Kanghwa
Imjin
*Mount Mani
(1,536 ft/468 m)*
▲ SEOUL ■
●
Inch'on
*Soraksan
National Park*
▲ *Mount Sorak
(5,604 ft /1,708 m)*

Taebaek Range

KANGWON

KYONGGI

NORTH
CH'UNGCH'ONG

Han

SOUTH
CH'UNGCH'ONG
Hahoe
● ● Andong

*Yellow
Sea*

Kum

Taejon ●

Sobaek Range

NORTH
KYONGSANG

Naktong

Taegu
●
● Kyongju

NORTH
CHOLLA

SOUTH
KYONGSANG

● Ulsan

N
↑

Kwangju
●

Somjin

▲ *Mount Chiri
(6,283 ft/1,915 m)*
● Pusan

SOUTH
CHOLLA

National Boundary
Province Boundary
- - - DMZ
■ Capital
● City
River

Hauido —

JAPAN

SOUTH
KOREA

Korea Strait

Cheju
●
▲ CHEJU
*Mount Halla
(6,398 ft / 1,950 m)*

Above: In traditional Korean villages, these posts are used to ward off evil spirits.

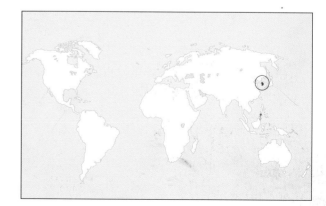

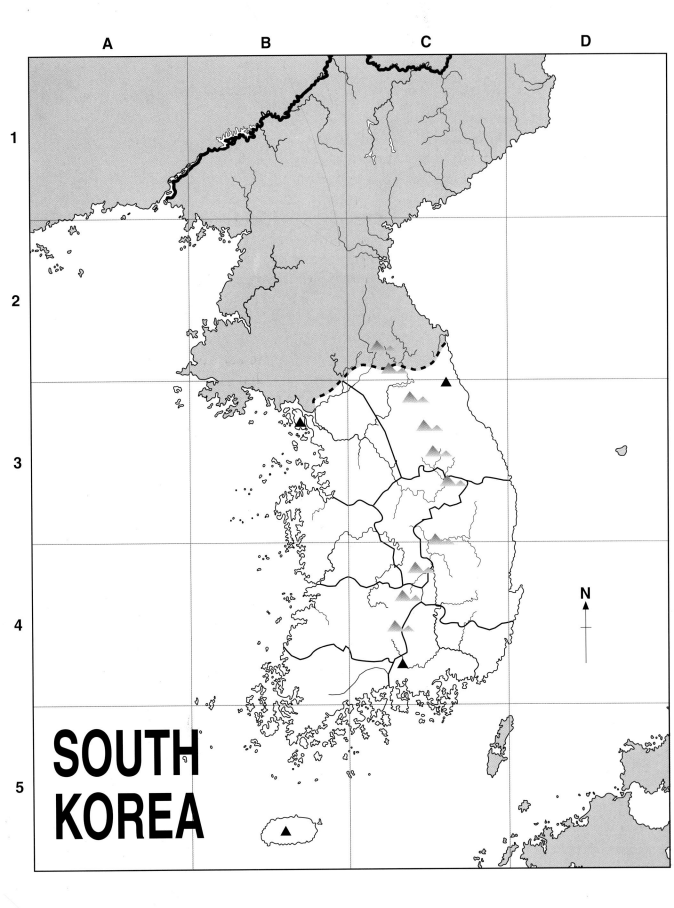

SOUTH
KOREA

How Is Your Geography?

Learning to identify the main geographical areas and points of a country can be challenging. Although it may seem difficult at first to memorize the locations and spellings of major cities or the names of mountain ranges, rivers, deserts, lakes, and other prominent physical features, the end result of this effort can be very rewarding. Places you previously did not know existed will suddenly come to life when referred to in world news, whether in newspapers, television reports, other books and reference sources, or on the Internet. This knowledge will make you feel a bit closer to the rest of the world, with its fascinating variety of cultures and physical geography.

Used in a classroom setting, the instructor can make duplicates of this map using a copy machine. (PLEASE DO NOT WRITE IN THIS BOOK!) Students can then fill in any requested information on their individual map copies. Used one-on-one, the student can also make copies of the map on a copy machine and use them as a study tool. The student can practice identifying place names and geographical features on his or her own.

Below: **Korean schoolchildren take a break from hiking to enjoy the breathtaking view.**

South Korea at a Glance

Official Name   Republic of Korea

Capital   Seoul

Official Language   Korean (hangul)

Population   47,904,370

Land Area   37,900 square miles (98,161 square km)

Provinces   Cheju, Kangwon, Kyonggi, North Cholla, North Ch'ungch'ong, North Kyongsang, South Cholla, South Ch'ungch'ong, South Kyongsang

Autonomous Cities   Inch'on, Kwangju, Pusan, Seoul, Taegu, Taejon, Ulsan

Highest Point   Mount Halla 6,398 feet (1,950 m)

Main Rivers   Han, Imjin, Kum, Naktong, Somjin

Main Religions   Buddhism, Christianity, Confucianism, shamanism

Ethnic Groups   Korean, Chinese

Major Holidays   New Year's Day (January 1)

                          Buddha's Birthday (April/May)

                          Children's Day (May 5)

                          Liberation Day (August 15)

Major Exports   Clothing, electronic products, fish, footwear, machinery and equipment, motor vehicles, ships, steel, textiles

Major Imports   Electronics and electronic equipment, grains, machinery, oil, organic chemicals, steel, textiles, transportation equipment

Currency   Won (1,324.5 KRW = U.S. $1 as of 2002)

Opposite: **The Changdok Palace in Seoul was added to the Kyongbok Palace in 1405.**

Glossary

Korean Vocabulary

bulgogi (bull-go-gee): grilled, marinated beef that is mixed with rice and wrapped in a lettuce leaf.

chajonnori (chah-john-nor-ee): a game in which two teams compete to knock their opponents off raised platforms.

changgi (chahng-gee): Korean chess.

changgo (chahng-go): an hourglass drum.

chima (chee-mah): a long, full, high-waisted wraparound skirt.

chogori (cho-gore-ee): a short jacket or blouse with long, full sleeves that ties in the front.

Chonwang (chong-wang): "King of Heaven"; the title that Hwanung, the son of the divine creator, gave himself.

daeryun (die-ryoung): competition.

dojang (doh-jahn): a gymnasium or training hall.

dongchae (dong-chay): a raised platform made of wood and old rice stalks that is used when playing chajonnori.

galbi (gall-bee): barbecued short ribs.

haenyo (hen-yo): female divers who live on Cheju.

hanbok (hahn-bock): traditional Korean clothing.

hangul (hahn-gool): the official written language of South Korea.

Harubang (hah-roo-bong): large statues carved out of lava stones.

hwarangdo (hwah-rang-doh): knights of the Korean military.

hyung (he-young): a basic component of taekwondo training known as form.

insam (in-sum): ginseng.

kat (cot): a traditional type of Korean hat.

kayagum (kie-yah-goom): a twelve-stringed zither.

kimchi (kim-chee): a spicy pickled salad.

kimjang (kim-jon): the period of time during which women made kimchi.

komungo (koh-moon-go): a six-stringed instrument that has sixteen movable bridges.

kyukpa (kee-yuk-pah): a basic component of taekwondo training known as breaking.

napa (nah-pah): a type of kimchi made of Chinese cabbage with turnips, radishes, cucumbers, and salted fish or shrimp.

ondol (on-doll): a heating system that warms the floors in a Korean home.

paduk (pah-duke): Korean checkers.

paji (pah-jee): baggy pants that are gathered at the ankles.

panchen (pahn-chen): side dishes that accompany a main course.

pansori (pahn-sore-ee): folktales.

sijo (see-joe): a type of short, lyrical poem.

Solnal (sole-nahl): New Year.

t'aegukki (tie-gook-ee): the national flag of South Korea.

Taejonggyo (tie-jahng-gee-oh): a religion centered around the worship of Tangun.

tal (tall): Korean masks.

talchum (tall-choom): mask dances.

Tangun (tahn-goon): the legendary father of Korea; also National Foundation Day.

yangban (yahng-bahn): the Korean upper class during the Choson dynasty.

English Vocabulary

abdicated: renounced or relinquished a throne, office, right, or responsibility, especially in a formal manner.

annexed: incorporated into the domain of a city, country, or state.

arable: suitable for farming.

boycotted: joined together to stop or prevent dealings with a country, group, or person, as a means of protest.

brocades: fabric woven with an elaborate raised design.

contingents: groups of people representing a country or organization at a meeting or other event.

curriculum: course of study.

deciduous: shedding leaves each year during a particular season.

dialect: a form or variation of a language spoken in a certain region or by a certain group of people.

elixir: a substance believed to be capable of prolonging life indefinitely.

etched: engraved.

hermit: a person who lives in solitude, away from others.

homogeneous: composed of parts or elements that are similar or the same.

humanities: the study of literature, languages, art, etc., as opposed to the study of sciences.

hydroelectricity: electric power generated from the force of water.

inciting: encouraging; urging on.

indelible: memorable; unforgettable.

longevity: a long duration of life.

martial law: law imposed by state military forces in response to civil unrest.

minstrels: medieval poets, singers, and musicians.

monsoon: a season of very heavy rainfall.

orchestrate: arrange, coordinate, or manipulate the elements to achieve a goal or effect.

Paleolithic: characteristic of the earliest phase of the Stone Age, which began in about 2,000,000 B.C.

peninsula: a body of land almost entirely surrounded by water.

penultimate: next to the last.

potent: powerful; producing powerful physical or chemical effects.

quince: a small tree that bears hard, fragrant, yellowish fruit used mainly for making jelly or preserves.

remnants: traces; remaining pieces.

sage: an extremely wise person.

secular: not relating to or concerned with religion.

skirmishes: brief encounters or fights between troops and a small group of people.

stamina: strength or power to endure fatigue or stress; endurance.

steep: soak in water or another liquid to soften, cleanse, or extract a substance.

tactician: one who is skilled at inventing and carrying out plans.

truce: agreement to end hostility or fighting between two parties.

typhoons: violent storms.

unfathomable: incomprehensible.

zither: a plucked instrument that consists of two sets of strings stretched over a flat box.

More Books to Read

Chi-Hoon: A Korean Girl. Patricia McMahon (Boyd's Mills Press)

Cooking the Korean Way. Okwha Chung and Judy Monroe (Lerner)

The Girl-Son. Adventures in Time series. Anne E. Neuberger (Carolrhoda Books)

Kim Dae-Jung. World Leaders Past and Present Series. Norm Goldstein and Arthur M. Schlesinger Jr, ed. (Chelsea House)

Korea. Cultures of the World series. Jill Dubois (Benchmark Books)

Korea. True Book series. Elaine Landau (Children's Press)

A Single Shard. Linda Sue Park (Houghton Mifflin)

South Korea. Major World Nations series. Patricia Shepheard (Chelsea House)

South Korea in Pictures. Visual Geography series. William H. Mathews, ed. (Lerner)

Things Korean. O-Young Lee and John Holstein (translator) (Charles E. Tuttle Co.)

Videos

Hidden Korea. (PBS Home Video)

Korea. (TMW/Media Group)

Korea: Ancient Treasure, Modern Wonder. (Master Communications Group)

South Korea: Land of Morning Calm. (IVN Entertainment)

Web Sites

korea.insights.co.kr/english/index.asp

www.lifeinkorea.com

www.media.granite.k12.ut.us/Curriculum/korea/

Due to the dynamic nature of the Internet, some web sites stay current longer than others. To find additional web sites, use a reliable search engine with one or more of the following keywords to help you locate information about South Korea. Keywords: *celadon pottery, Korean mask dance, Korean War, Kim Dae Jung, South Korea, Tangun.*

Index